adventures in the
Blue Beast

adventures in the Blue Beast

by Jeannie Morris

Rand McNally & Company
Chicago   New York   San Francisco

Library of Congress Cataloging in Publication Data

Morris, Jeannie.
  Adventures in the Blue Beast.

1. Europe—Description and travel—1971-
2. Morris, Jeannie. I. Title.
D923.M67   914′.04′550924   75-16275
 ISBN 0-528-81016-2

First printing, 1975

Foreword

I've got this wife who has ideas coming out of her in such a regular fashion that if I could convert them to a diarrhetic I could make a fortune selling Morris's little poop pills.

It was her idea to drop everything and take this one-year trip, and her idea to write about it. I remember the first time I saw Jeannie; we were both at the University of California at Santa Barbara. I was leaning over a girl friend's left arm trying to copy her English exam when this little mite of a chick went scuttling by the window of the classroom. She had on a bathing suit and was headed for the beach with a load of books under her arm. An hour later I saw her scuttling back. I thought she might be cute if she'd slow down, take the wiggle out of her walk, and stop looking so damn serious.

It was more than five years later, after we'd both done a lot of growing up, that we found each other again. We've been together ever since.

We're both 38 now. We've invested a lot in our family and we've enjoyed some great moments. Over the years, it seemed as though I'd never had enough time with my family—which is perhaps the reason we always got along so well. Well, this trip put it all together, and we get along now better than ever. Though the trip is over and we've more or less picked up our lives where we left off, we'll never be the same.

And like I said, it was Jeannie's idea. She's got a darn good brain for a girl with a wiggle in her tail.

Johnny Morris

For Bottsy and John

Contents

adventures in the Blue Beast

Onward!

Before we left, people down at NBC-TV's Chicago studios were laying bets that "The Flanker" would never go through with it. That's what they call Johnny around station WMAQ, The Flanker. At the time I wouldn't take those bets, because up until the last I wasn't altogether sure of Johnny's determination. That's one of the difficult-but-nice things about being married to a former All-Pro pass receiver: You can't cover him because you never know which way he's going to make his move.

It seems to be a common belief that no man could stand being cooped up with his wife and four kids for a whole year, that "today's man needs his work," thrives on it, in fact. Nonsense. Big-business propaganda. But even a sensible jock like Ron Santo went so far as to draw me aside and warn most sincerely that, in his opinion, not only would we learn to hate our kids, but that so much togetherness might put an irreparable strain on our marriage. As a professional athlete Ronnie should have known better; any marriage that can survive a decade in the National Football League can survive anything.

There were a number of people who agreed with Santo's view, but most looked upon our trip as the realization of a practically universal dream. Still, they invariably added, "Where do you get the guts to do it?" Naturally, I realize that few families are lucky enough to be able to scrape up the scratch for a venture such as ours; but that seemed to be beside the point. The fear so often mentioned first involved the unknowns which might be encountered in foreign lands; but even more important seemed to be the misgivings about disrupting life at home. We thought long and hard about these and other possible negatives, and maybe we were naive, but in the end we swallowed that beer commercial that says, "You only go around once in life, so grab all the gusto you can." And frankly, we were never aware of exercising anything as lofty as "courage."

Departure Day marked almost five years since I had signed up to write my first football column and brought home my first $50. I was liberated. (Liberation. That means you get to work for pay in addition to being housemaid, cook, chauffeur, Brownie leader, veterinarian, and so on.) Anyhow, that first $50 went into an account labeled "The Freedom Fund." And although my career expectations were minimal at the time, the family agreed that all my paychecks would go into The Fund since, fortunately, we were able to live comfortably on Johnny's salary. I was determined that The Freedom Fund would liberate us all. Before the balance had passed $500, I had begun to lobby for "The Plan." At the time I didn't know it would be a five-year plan. But even though we had five years to tamper with it, The Plan never lost its original simplicity: We would go to Europe and spend a year going wherever we happened to feel like going, doing whatever we happened to feel like doing.

Like our decision to buy a small farm and move out of the insular Chicago suburb of Winnetka, our resolution to travel with the children grew from a conviction that too many factors in our environment were leading to the dissolution of families. And this was happening at a time when the family was needed more than ever as a touchstone for both humanity and individuality. We saw the break-up everywhere. Some time ago, Johnny discovered along with me that our kids were the best people we knew, that taking them out to dinner on a Saturday night beat hell out of going to a cocktail party. We belonged to each other; and Johnny and I, knowing that this richness would fill only a short space in the lives of all of us, determined to make the most of it.

Somewhere I must insert a disclaimer about the role of my children in this narrative, and I guess this is as good a place as any. Think for a moment about the problems involved if *you* had to write a one-year chronicle of your activities and those of your children—that *they* would read. Pick any year—pick your *best* year—you'd have to be careful, right? Now, Johnny says I spoil the kids, that I overpraise them and overmassage their egos, and certainly in this narration you won't find me dwelling on their faults (or mine or Johnny's either, for that matter). So I won't be offended if you don't believe me when I tell you that all four of our children really are wonderful people. . . . They are, though.

The timing of our trip was determined when we woke up one morning and discovered that we had reached two optimums. For one, the children were the right ages: Holly, the youngest, would soon be 8, and Dan, pushing 17, would shortly be on his own; Tim and Debbie were almost 11 and 15. And The Freedom Fund was up to $30,000.

The big problem was to pry The Flanker loose from WMAQ-TV (alias NBC, alias RCA). Bob Lemon, the man who had originally hired Johnny away from pro football but had recently retired, had often told us that one was a fool to be loyal to a corporation, that loyalties properly belonged only with individuals, whether family or professional colleagues. We agreed. And our fellow workers at NBC thought we had one hell of an idea.

But for the far-off conglomerate we presented a real dilemma. Naturally, the station was involved in a ratings battle (they always are). It is just NBC's luck, if not especially mine, that Johnny is a great attraction for that superconsumer, the 18- to 49-year-old woman. The higher the proportion of these women that watch your programs, the more impressed the advertisers, the bigger the profits.

The second factor would apply to almost any guy in the country who might want to do what Johnny did, and this factor deals with the corporate machine. How long would our giant businesses last if any old cog could just take off for a year and expect to get his job back? Fortunately, Johnny's humble enough to know he's a corporate cog. But he doesn't want to be. Who does?

His cog-ness was about to be tested one day shortly after our intentions went public. Since being "liberated" into television and journalism, I had learned a little about the competitive pressure that used to be referred to as "a man's world," so I went along nervously with The Flanker as he was summoned to NBC's 20th floor executive suite.

Our general manager was new to the station and one of those fellows who was a lot bigger behind his desk than when he got up to shake your hand. He must have known that, because he stayed back there to deliver one of the most extraordinary dissertations I have ever heard, filled with cajolery, veiled bribes, and threats of vague "theys" in New York who "just won't have this." The man was scary and convincing. Faces of friends who'd been sucked in, chewed up, and spit out by the corporate machinery floated before us. When we walked out, I fully expected my beleaguered husband to say something like, "What do you think, Jeannie, could we be throwing it all away?" What Johnny said was, "Have you ever heard so much bullshit in all your life?"

Like I said, flankers are unpredictable.

After several consultations with our school district, it was agreed that Johnny would tutor Holly and Tim through their third and fifth grade work. Deb and Dan, on the other hand, became dropouts. They would simply be a high-school freshman and a junior one year later in their lives.

So we traded our two cars for a camper and rented the house fully furnished to a man who decided to pay us the year's rent in advance; in view of the inflation we subsequently encountered, this was a big break for us and our Freedom Fund. We carried the contents of closets and drawers to the basement, where we stored our personal effects on two-by-four slats in case of flood and installed a dehumidifier to thwart the damp. Into the empty spaces of our sparkling new Ford Econoline Camping Van we packed six cups, plates, and place settings of silverware; a camp cook kit; assorted film equipment and auto parts; a typewriter; six baseball gloves and a bat; and "The Duke," our football. Nothing to it, really.

We took a day or so to pack only our most comfortable clothes in six canvas duffle bags purchased at Sears, put the keys under the mat for the new tenant, and in August, 1973, took off.

Of course I'm oversimplifying. We oversimplified for a year. It felt SO good.

Beginning with Bugs

We had various motives for taking the *Queen Elizabeth II* from New York to Southampton, England. We knew, for one, that a luxury-liner crossing in the Old Style was soon to be a thing of the past. Furthermore, unlike many ships, the *Queen* had a hold large enough for the camper, making it possible for our van-home and its dwellers to arrive in Europe together. But mostly, we just wanted a chance to wind down between winding up our affairs in Chicago and starting the new life we would lead in Europe. The best result of the voyage across the Atlantic was summed up by Debbie when she said, "If I hadn't seen that water going by day after day, I would never have known how far away Europe was."

Taking the QE2 was like traveling *on* Britain *to* Britain. It gave us a chance to get accustomed to the class system which, despite reports to the contrary, is alive if not well.

The first and most expensive mistake we made during our entire year became evident one day out of port. We'd let ourselves be sold by a travel agent on the idea that when traveling by ship, first class was an absolute must. We got the impression that anything less was steerage. Nonsense. First class proved restrictive and even, in a sense, underprivileged. Not only did the dress standards require us to pack clothes which we would not need for the remainder of the year, but first class passengers were excluded from winning all the big pots in the afternoon bingo games! Furthermore, the ship's important facilities are open to all passengers; everyone ignores the "First Class Only" signs that abound. And moreover, first class is really not first, after all, because there's a "deluxe" class—and *that's* where the captain sits down to dinner with the world's princes, magnates, and movie stars. I never checked it out, but I'll bet deluxe passengers didn't even get to *play* bingo.

It was on the *Queen* that Holly discovered something our year's life-style would prove again and again: "It must be boring to be rich."

Dinnertime was the highlight of the day—although the food was not as fancy as the dining room. Dressed in our best duds, we'd move as inconspicuously as possible past the sedate crowd to our round table for six in the far, far corner of the blue-and-crystal room. Then The Flanker and Tim, who was always starving, would begin cocking eyebrows, raising arms, and otherwise signaling for the services of our waiter for the week, "Big John."

Big John was the most totally incompetent and thoroughly amusing waiter we had ever encountered. He was 6 feet 3 inches tall, his name was John McLaughlin, and he spoke in cockney spiced with gentry or gentry spiced with cockney, depending on his mood. We called him Big John in order to distinguish him from his friend "Little John." John Perry Jones, a 5-foot 7-inch Welshman, tended the next dining station, but spent much of his time bailing Big John out of his inevitable screw-ups before our table captain (the local overseer) caught him. Big John was always on the verge of having to walk the plank.

Early on we joined the Johns in antipathy to our table captain, a cocky little man spilling over with acquired snobbery, who'd alienated us by suggesting archly that the kids eat earlier, during the "Children's Hour," leaving Johnny and me "free to enjoy your meal."

Big John's service was characterized mainly by his absence in time of need, and it wasn't long before we concluded that he was nipping in the pantry. But most of the time he at least managed to be on the spot to take our order, feigning dignity while the captain tried to look over his shoulder.

Then came suspense time: What would we be served and which to whom? Usually Big John would give Holly, whom he insisted upon calling Polly, whatever he thought was good for her. Everybody else's meal he mixed up, delivering each dish with a comment on the quality of the ingredients or the character of the cook. As soon as Big John left for the kitchen, we'd switch our plates around until everyone got at least approximately what he'd ordered; then we'd call Little John to fill in the gaps. There was so much food that none of us went away dissatisfied. But we sometimes left the table with stomachaches—from laughing.

Several weeks later we visited Little John on his mother's tiny, ancient farm in Wales near Llanfairpwllgwyngyllgogerychwyrndrobwll-llantysiliogogogoch, the village with the longest name in the world. Every night on the ship Holly had made Little John pronounce the name of his village in Old Welsh. Little John told us that at the time he'd left the *Queen* for his furlough on the farm, Big John was still up to his old tricks, but surviving.

We were grateful to both men for knocking the stuffiness out of the *Queen*. At least John McLaughlin and John Jones understood that a "Children's Hour" had no place in a "children's" year.

Having never traveled out of the States before and having no idea where to go once off the boat, we'd had our travel agent make one week of reservations for us in and around England. The first of these dates was in Exeter at the Royal Clarence, which is not what you'd call your upbeat hotel. In fact, I now know, it was "veddy, veddy" (which is to say, extremely) British. Thereafter we tried to avoid such hotels, not because we didn't like them, but because they didn't seem to like us (read: children).

The Royal Clarence was the most charming hotel I had ever seen, located across from the historic Exeter Cathedral on what must be the quietest square in Europe. The pigeons even cooed extra quietly. The Clarence didn't have bellboys or even bellmen, but they had bell-grampas and bellgreatgrampas, the kind where you instinctively reach for his burden and say, "Here, sir, let me help you." On our second day there, the hotel manager asked Tim if he would like a job carrying luggage for a tour group that was expected shortly. We were pleased when Tim bounded into our room after a long absence to tell us he had a job. We thought he'd been out feeding the pigeons. But shortly before the buses were to arrive, he was fired—for "running" through the lobby. How could Tim explain to the head bellgrampa that, although he'd been warned to behave with decorum, the run was his normal gait?

We'd planned to stay at the Royal Clarence for three nights, but on the second, Deb's need for a T-shirt she had left out in the camper short-circuited our plans. "Throw it to me," stage-whispered Deb, leaning out her third-floor window as she spied Dan crossing the moonlit square with her shirt.

"NO!" Johnny and I breathed (too late) from the fourth-floor window just above Deb. Dan's lob carried the white bit of fluff up over the first floor, where it settled on the awning that covered the formal front entrance of the hotel. He couldn't let it lie there. Walking sedately through the lobby, then dashing up the stairs, Dan found an empty room with an open window leading onto a ledge that ran across the front of the Royal Clarence. As we all watched from above, Dan emerged onto the ledge. At about the same time, a bellgrampa stepped out of the red-carpeted entrance and, craning his neck, asked, "I beg your pardon, but what are you about, young man?"

White curtains fluttered in our suddenly empty windows while Dan, stretched out on his belly, snatched the T-shirt from the awning, slithered back into the hotel, and beat it upstairs.

The next morning we were asked to leave the Royal Clarence.

We got to Ireland via car ferry across the Irish Sea from Swansea in Wales. After less than a week on the road, we'd already given up such travel traditions as "planning ahead" and "reservations." So we stopped at the Swansea terminal to check departure times before seeking a hotel where we could wash, eat, and rest prior to boarding the ferry. However, at the terminal we discovered that the only ship in the next two days would be sailing in four hours—and it was fully booked. If we were to have any chance at all of getting aboard, we would have to "stand by." We were hardly up to a four-hour wait (possibly fruitless) followed by a twelve-hour voyage, but we doggedly pulled our van into the line of other hopefuls. As it turned out, there was plenty of room for us people, though the camper was the only standby vehicle to make it aboard.

We should have missed the boat.

At first there was no hint that we were in for anything but a fair sea voyage. The warnings we'd heard about the wild Irish Sea appeared ridiculous at best. It was August and warm, and as night fell the stars were magnificent. We got some food in the snack bar and, with our sleeping bags, were prepared to curl up in third class chairs in a vast room that, because of the contours of the ship, resembled a theatre. The floor even sloped.

There was no stage, however, and the "house" was packed with what might generously be termed a rude audience. Everyone was either munching, snoring, laughing, or drinking. Later we were to become accustomed to—indeed, to fit right in with—such a crowd; but on this night we agreed with Tim, who said it was a lousy show. He said he'd found a better place on deck that was protected from the wind. As we filed out of the cabin, we passed three ruddy women who'd found shelter in deck chairs under the overhang; one nudged me and said, "You'll be back, love."

By 9 o'clock the six of us were snuggled under the stars, seeing vividly why men of the sea find the heavens both guide and companion. With the throb of the ship's huge engines playing bass to the sound of the sloshing sea, we were asleep in minutes.

At midnight it began to rain. And it blew. We gathered up our sleepy kids and wet bags and dashed down under the second deck, which was by now crowded with others who had craved fresh air but wisely scorned the stars. The Irish ladies in their dry wool blankets looked us right in our distressed faces and laughed.

Back in the "theatre" we found four empty chairs. Tim and I stretched out on the floor on damp sleeping bags. I was just drifting off again when I began to realize that the three very drunk people in the chairs above and to the rear of me were discussing my anatomy.

The girl was daring one of the two men to kick me! Was I dreaming? A good deal of laughter and then (thump!) a swift blow to my left bun. I jumped up and turned to see them stifling giggles and passing the bottle. Johnny was sleeping quietly on the other side of the aisle. Should I ask him to avenge my honor (or should I ask them for a drink)? "The hell with it," I thought, and gave up to exhaustion.

Four hours later we arrived in Cork and in three days found the Connemara country, where the yen to settle into our new way of life finally hit us. We'd been traveling steadily since landing at Cork. We'd stayed in Killarney and Tipperary, but it was in Galway that someone suggested that we continue on to the sea.

From Galway we went to Oughterard, the town that stands at the entrance to the Connemara country. In Oughterard we bought the few things we needed to rig the van for camping. Then, traveling roughly northwest, we passed the miles of peat bog, sheep range, and occasional forest land. The mountains that characterized the West Country were more craggy than huge; the creeks were crystal clear and the "loughs," or lakes, plentiful. The grass was the greenest green we'd ever seen.

The road we chose led us through the heart of the Mountains of Connemara; past Maam Cross and Recess; down the Inagh Valley, where Twelve Pins Mountain towered; through Kylemore and Tully Cross; and thence to Lettergesh. The moment we crested a green velvet hill and looked upon the wild Atlantic coast of Ireland, we knew it was time to rest. It was on the sea near Lettergesh that we saw pinned to a farmer's barn a wooden sign that read "camping."

I never figured out whether our farmer kept his cattle away from us or us from them, but we were confined to one pasture and the animals another. As neighbors, we and the beasts lived much the same. But while the sheep and cows were fenced in on four sides, our pasture was open to 200 yards of gleaming beach uninterrupted by rocks, seaweed, or even a single footprint, and boasted cold running water and four flushing toilets. Only one toilet was unlocked each day, however—an efficiency measure, I suppose, because there were never any more than four families sharing our ten-acre emerald carpet at any one time.

Our spot, some 20 paces from the beach, was a dip in the earth which 30 years before might have been a gun emplacement but was now a lush nest with three gently sloping sides, while the fourth side was open and facing the sea. Against his better judgment, Johnny let Deb and me talk him into pulling the camper into this natural shelter—with The Dad swearing all the time that we'd never get out. We did, though, five days later.

Although Connemara might have been the cleanest place we'd ever lived in, our main problem—that is to say, my main problem— was dirt. Up to this time, we had spent only one night in the camper; and since we planned a lot more camping in the coming months, I wanted to get us off to a good start. So I preached that high morale came from doing things right, keeping the van neat, and eating well. There is a powerful temptation to bum it when you're camping. For people who have been relatively prosperous all their lives, camping is a pleasant way to learn how easily poverty can result in apathy. Ordinary tasks require extraordinary effort.

For example, according to my diary, this is how one morning went:

6:00 A.M.   Why are sunrises fresher than sunsets? The colors are the same. I am sitting on a tuft of turf 100 yards up the beach from the campsite. No one is stirring except our neighbors, the cattle, and two of them have broken out and are moseying along in the sand. They seem afraid of the surf. The air is tonic. Only sounds: the sea, sheep, cows, waterbirds; I hear no machinery, no tractors, trucks, cars—and we haven't seen a jet streak since entering Connemara. In the early sunlight even the centuries-old stone farmhouses look young again.

12:30 P.M.   I haven't accomplished a thing and I've only just sat down for the first time in four and a half hours! Is this the way it's going to go for a whole entire year? Witness:

Dying for a cup of coffee, I return to the camper at 8:00 A.M. I can't do much more than pivot in front of the sink with all of the cots up, so I try to get everybody awake. It's not easy. The air is so good for sleeping. As each guy arises, he or she pitches a sleeping bag and pillow out onto the tarpaulin that is stretched over the dewy grass. I put the coffee on while the boys stow the hammocks. Debbie pours cereal, I make toast with forks over one burner while Tim scrambles eggs. In between I'm trying to move the laundry into one pile and straighten the van. Naturally, we are walking all over each other. By 9:30 we sit down to a breakfast that tastes fantastic. We sit and talk over the table for a whole hour. Then Tim and Holly go after a bucket of water which I put on to heat. Debbie is to wash the dishes. But Deb and Dan both disappear, and Tim reports that they are dancing on the beach . . . peculiar, but I never check it out. Presently Deb returns. After she finishes the dishes, I wash some towels, hanging them to dry over the struts that hold up the canopy. Meanwhile, Johnny, Holly, and Tim are rolling up the sleeping bags.

Finishing the wash, I grab my cosmetic kit and soap and run 100 yards up the pasture to the john and the community sink. I have an outdoor, cold water wash and, as J. C. ("Sweetline") Caroline used to say, "it hurts so-o-o good." I come back and hang a mirror on a hook, fix my face and hair, sweep out the camper, and sit down for my second cup of coffee over the typewriter. One sip and two paragraphs later, Dan runs in from the beach. "What's for lunch?" he asks. I look at my watch and it's noon. Unbelievable.

Although we grew more efficient as time went on and there was more sharing of the tasks, this is more or less the way it went for the year. Camping is very time-consuming.

Besides the cattle and the sheep in this West Country of Ireland, there is such an animal as a Connemara pony. And on our second day there, Debbie and Tim went scouting for a ride. They had been gone for more than two hours when we spotted the kids astride a couple of hardy ponies, galloping down the beach toward us, Debbie's long, blond hair (well, Tim's too) blowing in the wind. They'd quickly found a farmer who would let them use the ponies; what had taken so long were the wild berry brambles beside the road. Their pockets were crammed with these ripe morsels—and I never did get the purple stains out of Tim's pants. But from then on and until we left Great Britain, we feasted at will on the plentiful wild berries.

On day three we ran out of food, so Johnny and I, after setting the kids to their lessons, took two canvas backpacks and embarked upon the first of many hitchhiking expeditions (The Flanker wasn't about to try to pull the camper out of its nest for mere food).

The nearest town of any size was Kylemore, but as it was past noon, the butchers' counters were bare and the grocers' shelves meagerly stocked. We were able to buy sausage and bacon, fresh bread, rice, and tomatoes. We loaded our packs and hiked back. From our farmer we would get milk and eggs.

Shopping for food isn't much fun anywhere in the United Kingdom. You need strong legs, good wind, a lot of patience, and your own shopping bag as you move from one small store to another, filling the family's needs. This makes for "charm," of course, but I'll take my charm in restaurants and antique shops, not grocery stores. With our appetites, it was particularly inconvenient that milk never came in any container (except a cow) larger than a pint. Compared to the rest of Western Europe, Britain is curiously backward in many ways. And Ireland, in addition, is poor. Nowhere did we see more meat on the hoof and less on the hook.

Nevertheless, we began in Ireland what was to become not the least of our adventures—an adventure in eating. Wherever we traveled we managed creative concoctions from available ingredients, though even with "prepared" foods it wasn't always easy. On one occasion a few weeks after we left Ireland, Holly insisted on pudding for dessert. Dan, who served as chief translator, consulted a Finnish-English dictionary to make the following translation of the recipe on the back of a box of chocolate pudding mix:

INSTRUCT WITH PUDDING POWDER

1. Mix powder for pudding with 40 grams (2 spoons) sugar.
2. Subtract from ½ liter cold milk 6 spoons and good stir with pudding with sugar blend.
3. Leavings milk dejected, make way with heat and pestering him inspect powder for pudding then, along with blend kitchen one to two minutes.
4. Hot pudding climb into on purpose holder and leave yes, cool itself and squeeze.

Using this guide—and a dash of previous experience—I was able to make Holly's chocolate pudding. As The Flanker put it to Deb and me after finishing lunch by the road a few miles out of Budapest, Hungary, "You two are real champs at making chicken salad out of chicken [bleep]."

Leaving Kylemore after our shopping tour, Johnny and I spotted something far more interesting than food: an announcement that the next day (Sunday) would be the 86th annual running of the Renvyle Games. Renvyle was a village about eight miles from Lettergesh ... which meant we'd *have* to pull the camper out. For such a fundamental essential as sport, Johnny proved willing. We got our van out with only two of us pushing.

What a track meet the Renvyle Games proved to be! It seemed everybody in the whole county was there—and so many of them red-haired, blue-eyed, and freckled! (And so many of them loaded!) Not only was it one of the gayest and friendliest sports affairs we'd ever attended, it was also close to being the most well-organized track meet Johnny and I had seen—and we've been to quite a few. But I guess you learn something in 86 years.

The races were to last all day, and a fine day it was. The sun was shining, and the temperature was in the low 70s. The track was set in somebody's pasture, a depression surrounded by green and rocky hills. The events included a 56-pound shot put and a tug-of-war. And Johnny, pawing the ground like a restless stallion, asked had we come here just to spectate? Well, not Holly, anyway. She entered the 100-meter race for eight-year-old-and-under girls, finishing a strong second and winning a silver medal on a blue ribbon. We were so proud!

Meanwhile, I was growing apprehensive. I saw on the program that Renvyle included the "Big Stud" event, the 100-meter open for men 18 and over. We could see the 100 was going to be special even here, because the Irish lads, unlike their little brothers and sisters, were equipped with track shoes and shorts—and even school and club colors. Naturally, The Flanker decided to enter.

I hid. I knew Johnny was still fast, and his age didn't impress me as being much of a factor. Not that it's any more special than the fact that Dan, for instance, is a talented mechanic, but Johnny is a super athlete—and a compulsive competitor. Anyhow, he won, coasting, and the award was a beautiful trophy fashioned of Connemara marble and silver, the prettiest statuette Johnny had ever received.

To my mind, he stole it. After all, he was a "ringer," a pro—not to mention a foreigner.

The topper was the award ceremony. It was run out of an old Chevy, which served as a sound vehicle, and the awardees were to stand on a platform, just like in the Olympics. I'm telling you, the Renvyle Games were *big* in Connemara! So there they were (I was peeking out from behind a bunch of red-faced old fellas), the three of them, two very young men and Johnny. The announcer pronounced in a deep (and slightly drunken) brogue: "Third place goes to Sean O'Flannery of Toombeola [applause from the clan] . . . and in second, from Curraghreevagh, Timothy Mayo [great screams and cheers] . . . and our grand champion, winner of the first prize in the 100-meter dash [a long pause], Johnny Morris [and in falling tones], U. . . . S. . . . A." [Silence] I died.

Do you remember how, in "The Wild One," Marlon Brando strapped his gold motorcycle trophy on the handles of his bike to signify his macho leadership? Well, The Flanker set his "silver" on the dash of the camper, right beside the copper replica of Chicago's Picasso sculpture that our friends at NBC Sports had sent along as a reminder of home. And there the two statues rode for the remainder of our trip.

We had just turned onto the narrow track which led back to our campsite when the accident occurred. I'm not sure whether Johnny was admiring his silver statuette or scratching his fleabites when he drove into the ditch. He said it was the fleabites and so the whole disaster was therefore my fault.

Why? Well, we had camped one night out of Galway before reaching the sea at Lettergesh. We'd simply turned off the road onto a dirt path that led over a stream, beside a lake, and up the side of a forested mountain. Johnny suggested we camp by the stream. I suggested we camp on the mountainside. The kids had sided with me since—even though there wasn't another human soul in sight—it was more private, they said, to have the porta-pot set out between the van and a mountain than by a stream in the deep of a valley. Thus, the mountain won. But this lovely site, protected and offering an incredible view, was infested with a critter so tiny that it infiltrated the finely meshed screens that covered all of the camper's open windows. Johnny suffered. He has a mental thing and, I guess, a physical allergy to any kind of bug bite. He commenced to scratch . . . and was still scratching four days later.

At the time, the rest of us thought his preoccupation with bugs was pretty funny. But the nibbles grew into welts. And so, Johnny claimed, as he turned the van onto the skinny dirt road leading past the farmer's house and down to our camp by the beach, he was using most of his powers of concentration to scratch. Which is how *I* got us into the squishy ditch.

Dan, who as I said is a talented mechanic (which time and again proved fortunate), got out to appraise our predicament and informed us that the car was resting on the "muffler, front torsion bars, and rear axle." "What does that mean?" Johnny asked accusingly. "It means," replied Dan, "that the van's got to be lifted, not pulled, out of this ditch."

It was then that Johnny dubbed the camper "the Blue Beast."

While Dan supervised Tim and Holly in an effort to tote rocks from the fields to wedge around the sinking wheels, Deb and I, famished, stayed in the van and fixed dinner (at a 30-degree angle). Johnny went to find a farmer with a tractor or an ox or something! It was Sunday still, and we figured there might not be such a thing as a tow truck any closer than Galway.

As it turned out there weren't any farmers, either. They were still out celebrating the results of the Renvyle Games. But along about dark, with a smile and a rumble, a man with a big tractor lumbered in. The word of our predicament had spread to the kindly populace.

With all of us pushing and lifting (all except Holly, whom Dan somewhat nervously allowed to hold his camera and photograph the event), and the tractor pulling, we rescued the Beast. There were no visible injuries. Even the statuettes were still in place.

All Johnny could remember about The Night of the Irish Fleas was that it had been one long, miserable evening. For my part, I had thought it was pretty funny; after all, we had spent about two hours talking and laughing before Johnny really began to scratch. So, wishing to have a disinterested witness to testify that camping can be fun (and funny)—*and* to reestablish my own credibility—I decided to "bug" The Beast on another night, our second on the beach at Lettergesh. Unbeknownst to anyone, I rigged my tape recorder.

To set the scene: Debbie and I had just finished the dishes, and since the complete meal process, including post-dinner conversation, had taken over three hours, it was quite late. Deb, for one, was anxious to have Dan unstrap the sleeping cots and rig the super-structure so that she could go to sleep. For his part, Dan was trying to log the photos he'd taken during the past few days. Johnny had other preoccupations, as you will see. Mind you, it was only our third night of actually sleeping in the Beast. We had been staying in hotels before we got to Ireland, and it is an understatement to say that we hadn't quite got the camping routine down pat.

The following, then, is a transcribed portion of the "audio" of an evening in the camper. I leave the video to your imagination.

Johnny: Ah ha, nothing like a freshing up before you go to bed. I think we have to shut all the windows tonight.

Holly: Oh, Dad, the battery is going dead in this flashlight.

Jeannie: What do you need it for?

Tim: I'm *sure* it's not dead.

Debbie: Don't wiggle that mirror.

Dan: What day did we play golf? We took off Wednesday morning from Exeter, right? And was it Tuesday night that you guys went out to dinner?

Johnny: No, that was in Exeter . . . Oh, in Exeter. Yes.

Holly: Deb, I can't find your cosmetic kit. I know it's here, but I can't find it.

Debbie: OK. Don't worry about it. I'll wait till tomorrow morning when we can see.

Holly: I found Dan's. I found everybody's, but I can't find yours.

Debbie: Don't WORRY!

Tim: You give me that dumb flashlight and I know I can get it working.

Debbie: I wish you'd fix up those beds.

Tim: I know I can fix the flashlight and that is it . . . and that is it . . . Where is it?

Debbie: Mom . . . MOM! Can Dan put up the things now so we can go to bed?

Tim: Ple-e-ease, Mother, will you tell me where the flashlight is!

Debbie: Can he, Mom?

Dan: How come it's so much fun when we're on a budget? I like this.

Tim: Will you MOVE?

Debbie: Will he, Mom?

Jeannie: Will he what?

Debbie: Will he fix up the beds now? I want to go to sleep.

Dan: People are still standing up.

Debbie: Come on, Mom.

Johnny: We're starting to accumulate mosquitos in here.

Jeannie: Where's the flashlight?

Johnny: You'd better shut that door.

Jeannie: Mosquitos? There's no mosquitos.

Tim: Watch out, Dad! Right in front of your face!

Jeannie: There are no mosquitos on the seashore.

Johnny: There's one right *there*.

Jeannie: That's not a mosquito.

Dan: Well, kill that large animal!

Holly: What's that huge bug?

Jeannie: I have never seen a mosquito that big.

Johnny: If that's a mosquito, baby, I'm clearing out. (*General laughter*)

Holly: That *is* a mosquito, Dad.

Dan: That would leave your whole face a bite . . . It's called a crane fly. You know what that kind of creature does? It eats other flies.

Johnny: Well, I don't care.

Dan: Just remove it kindly and put it outside. (*Sound of door sliding*)

Debbie: Mom . . . MOTHER! Can Dan set up these things now. Can't I at least get up in bed? I want to get some sleep tonight.

Tim: The question is, where did we put the flashlight? I think I handed it to Dad.

Dan: Dad, what did you do with the flashlight?

Johnny: By God, we did get some bugs in here.

Tim: Dad, what did you do with that flashlight?

Debbie: Mother . . . MOTHER!

Dan: Look at the bug smeared all over the ceiling!

Tim: Where's the flashlight?

Johnny: I don't know where the flashlight is.

Debbie: Mother . . . Mother.

Tim: I wonder where it is?

Debbie: Mother . . . Mother?

Jeannie: That's my name, but you're wearing it out.

Debbie: Mother, will you please ask Dan to set up the things now?

Tim: Oh oh hum de da da. *(Tim hums, whistles, and sighs throughout most of the remainder of the tape.)*

Debbie: MOTHER!

Jeannie: Do you want them set up quite yet?

Johnny: Set up what?

Jeannie: Sling up Debbie's cot—so we still have one side to walk on.

Johnny: OK, just a second; just a few more bugs here.

Jeannie: Dan's gonna do it.

Johnny: Gotta shut these windows.

Holly: Mom. Timmy . . .

Johnny: See, this guy just got in . . . That's a fly, though. Shut it. Now. Quick!

Dan: What's the name of the hotel . . . ?

Holly: Is that a mosquito?

Johnny: Look at 'em! What ARE those?

Debbie: Just kill 'em and kill 'em now!! *(Slap, slap)*

Johnny: Not with your hands, you idiot! Use a piece of paper, they have germs all over them!

Jeannie: Germs? On a mosquito?

Holly: MOM! . . . Mom, look.

Dan: What's the name of that movie we saw?

Jeannie: "Live and Let Die."

Dan: Oh, that's right.

Jeannie: How could you forget?

Tim: On *any* mosquito you can find germs.

Johnny: Are all the doors and windows shut?

Jeannie: Does it hurt, Holly? Well, try this.

Debbie: Those little buggers come in through the screen . . . Oh, look at them!

Johnny: Those can't get in through the screen.

Debbie: Are you quite sure?

Johnny: Yeah, I'm sure. Listen, we've got to shut the doors earlier at night. We had the doors open and the lights on.

Debbie: Mom . . . Mom . . . Will you give me a warm wrap to wear tonight?

Jeannie: What part of your body do you want warm?

Dan: At least they can't get through the screen.

Debbie: Just my legs . . . and another shirt.

Jeannie: Another shirt.

Holly: *I* have a sweatshirt on and Dad's shirt on.

Debbie: How am I supposed to brush my teeth? With what?

Jeannie: All you do is this: I'll show you how to do it. You take a cup . . .

Debbie: Oh, it smells over here! Dad let one!

Dan: Did I take any pictures on this day?

Jeannie: It's something stale.

Debbie: It is not.

Tim: It does smell over there, Deb; you're quite right.

Johnny: What is that smell? I can't . . . a certain spot and you walk over there and it smells like garbage or something.

Dan: Brown water, the dishwater is brown.

Johnny: It was there last night.

Jeannie: Debbie, here's how you do it. You fill your cup . . .

Debbie: That's all right.

Jeannie: Debbie, *please* brush your teeth.

Debbie: Mom, they're clean enough. It's just disgusting.

Johnny: *You* think it is, but we all disagree.

Jeannie: We think it's disgusting if you don't brush your teeth.

Debbie: All right now, Dan, you're supposed to put up this bed now!

Dan: I'm not supposed to do anything. I might write on the back of your leg if you keep bothering me.

Debbie: Dad, will you make him?

Johnny: If you brush your teeth.

Debbie: Forget it.

Dan: Brush your teeth, then I'll do it.

Debbie: I'll brush my teeth in the morning.

Dan: Oh God, never mind, I'll do it. I don't want to get my head kicked.

Jeannie: Johnny, do you want to brush your teeth?

Johnny: I did.

Jeannie: In here? Did you spit in this?

Johnny: I took a cup and spit outside.

Dan: Spitting. Spitting is not good.

Jeannie: Oh yeah? It's good for your health sometimes.

Debbie: Mom, where are those pants that you said I could wear?

Jeannie: If I knew, I'd wear them myself.

Johnny: Oh oh, we've got to tighten this thing, this overhead brace.

Dan: Debbie's gonna be up there. It's OK.

Debbie: *Wait a second,* you better tighten that thing.

Tim: It's my side, Deb.

Debbie: Well, if that side goes, my side goes too.

Dan: I insist. Before we put these things up, this stove will be cleared.

Holly: It hurts.

Jeannie: Don't itch it. Does anybody else need warm water to wash with?

Dan: No. God, is it brown! What are you doing?

Jeannie: I'm going to wash now.

Tim: Don't lie to yourself, Dad *(Johnny is patting his stomach).* Dad's sitting there thinking to himself, "Oh, I'm skinny, I'm skinny, I'm skinny."

Johnny: Debbie, take it easy on that. Didn't Danny warn you last night? You jerked the brace right out of there.

Dan: You're fixing it if it breaks. And remember, you pull these things, the sidebars, and hang on to the strap while you pull them out.

Johnny: What is this stuff, Jeannie? Is this candy?

Holly: They're Sweet Tarts. I think they're Sweet Tarts ... Are they squarish?

Dan: Tim, you're going to have to get out of the way.

Tim: You're walking all over my sleeping bag.

Holly: Dad, they're Sweet Tarts.

Jeannie: Holly, stick this jacket into your bag and around your legs.

Dan: Timmy, don't go up there yet.

Johnny: Danny ... Danny ... Does that go like that every night? God, whoever sleeps up there is going to fall on us.

Jeannie: Johnny, that's the sturdiest thing in the world.

Johnny: I know *that's* sturdy. I'm not worried about that. I'm worried about these little slots. One of those slots breaking, that's all.

Tim: Will somebody please, please ... Will somebody please hand me my sleeping bag?

Dan: I'll get it.

Jeannie: Do you know which one of the two that look alike it is?

Tim: It doesn't matter, they're the same.

Jeannie: Yeah. But you don't want each other's cooties, do you?

Tim: Cooties!

Johnny: That's Tim's. I rolled his up.

Jeannie: From now on wrap up your own and you'll remember it. Last time Dan and Deb wrapped up everybody's sleeping bags.

Johnny: I think that's Dan's.

Dan: I can tell after you unroll them. You can't put anything up there yet. I have to take this bar out to put this bar in and I have to hold both of them in my hands. *(BANG! BANG! BANG!)*

Jeannie: Look! Johnny's chinning himself on it!

Debbie: Dad, you don't have enough trust. If it falls, we're the ones who'll get hurt. All those sharp objects to fall on. Look how it sags.

Dan: That's the suspension.

Johnny: OK. Upstairs, you guys.

Debbie: This is mine, *dahling.*

Tim: No, this is mine, *dahling.*

Jeannie: Does anybody have to go to the bathroom?

Tim: Deb, that's *my* side.

Jeannie: Put a little more air in it.

Johnny: OK, this is your bag, Timmy.

Dan: I have the one with the stuff hanging off, OK?

Johnny: OK.

Debbie: Tim, would you stop singing that song?

Dan: OK, UP, Tim-Buck.

Johnny: Where's my James Bond book?

Dan: It's in the bookcase.

Tim: You don't get a pillow when you're on the floor with the air mattress. Give it to me.

Dan: Well, wait. We can't change pillows.

Jeannie: We're one short. The guy with the air mattress doesn't get a pillow.

Dan: Puke. He's going to be all over my pillow?

Johnny: That's OK.

Dan: Gross. I want the case washed before I use it again.

Tim: OK. Who do you want of all these people to use your pillow?

Johnny: Not you, I guess.

Tim: Debbie.

Dan: No. She hasn't brushed her teeth.

Johnny: Up, Timmy. Help Timmy up.

Tim: I can get up. I'm not a baby.

Johnny: No. We don't want you hanging on there like that. Watch your head.

Jeannie: Anybody else have to go to the bathroom?

Debbie: It's too far. I'll go in the morning.

Jeannie: How can she do that?

Dan: Get the sand out of my face. Tim, your feet are sandy.

Tim: My feet aren't sandy. Dan, I'll do it myself. Dan, LET GO!

Dan: Ooh, God, they're so sandy.

Tim: Don't you love my feet, Dan?

Jeannie: Dan, is the back door unlocked so I can sneak out if I wake up early?

Dan: Now. Did I take any pictures that day?

Jeannie: What day?

Dan: This day . . . here, that I'm talking about.

Jeannie: You took pictures all day.

Dan: Not today. I'm talking about the last full day we spent in Exeter.

Jeannie: Dan, you've got to keep up better with your log.
Debbie: Be quiet! Holly's asleep!
  Dan: Mom ... Mom ... MOM ... Did I take any pictures that last day in Exeter?
Johnny: God ... there's another one ... Got 'im!

Naturally, we were dirty as well as exhausted after spending the day at dusty Renvyle and then undergoing the strenuous ordeal of lifting the Beast out of the ditch. Most European campgrounds have cold showers at the least, but our Connemara campground came equipped with only one good facility for cleansing the whole body: the Atlantic Ocean. We had put on our bathing suits, taken our soap and towels, and bathed in the salty sea twice before, but nobody felt like doing it again on this, our last evening there. So The Mom (I became "The Mom" when one day Dan decided that my achievements were important enough to merit a title)—The Mom agreed to give cold sponge baths. I would show them how it was done in a hospital. Everyone was willing to go along but Deb. She heated the water.

We had two big bath blankets, and with one on the bed and one on top of the volunteer I gave each a thorough scrubbing while the others waited in line. Just like in the hospital, the "washer" started at the extremities and worked toward the middle, turning over the cloth and soap to the "washee" to finish the most sensitive part of the job. It was late, and the campground so empty that we didn't bother to close the curtains. Finally snuggled into our bags at midnight, we got to laughing again when Deb commented that had anyone been watching through the windows they would have thought our family was really strange. We began to picture what our ménage must seem to someone on the outside looking in: The Beast rocking every time Johnny turned over (he's a flopper, not a turner); so many voices coming from such a small space—a little girl's and a big man's and all the sounds in between. "Just like the Waltons," Holly decided: "Dan-Boy," she asked, "which is stronger, a tractor or an ox or the Beast?"

"A tractor. Now go to sleep."

"Dad, Tim keeps putting his feet in my face," said Debbie.

"I told you to put your heads in the same direction." Johnny was growing impatient. "And Deb, when you shift around do it gently. Your cot is sagging about ten inches above my nose."

"Don't *anyone* say what you're thinking about Dad's nose," Tim piped up.

"Now just SETTLE DOWN AND GO TO SLEEP, DAMMIT," said The Dad (with a flop).

Well, not exactly like the Waltons.

That night our first storm came up, and the rain and wind were fierce. Our home was so tight and dry and warm that it was a pleasure to intermittently doze and wake up, listening to the wind blow. And so the Beast was baptized.

"Ireland, sir, for good or evil," George Bernard Shaw once said, "is like no other place under Heaven, and no man can touch its sod or breathe its air without becoming better or worse."

I think we became better. At least we felt ready to return to England and then to tackle the rest of Europe.

"Off We Go into the Wild Blue Yonder . . ."

I don't mind telling you London was a bit of a bust for us. It was our fault: We did it wrong. On the other hand, it was a good learning experience. By the time we hit Paris and Rome, Europe's other two congested capitals, we'd learned to find *good* cheap restaurants, to park the Blue Beast and use public transportation, and to pace our sightseeing according to the patience and attention spans of our two smallest denominators. Children have relatively limited culture absorption levels—especially when it comes to simply *viewing*, as, for example, at museums and galleries. *Participating* in a culture is something else again. Our kids eventually learned everything from bargaining in country markets to beating an octopus to death on the stones of a Cretan square (and then cooking and eating it, of course). Now *that* is culture absorption.

In cities, where there is always too much to see and do that is essentially nonparticipatory, we had to learn to choose not necessarily what was the most educational, enlightening, or erudite amongst cultural pursuits, but whatever we thought the kids could identify with and thus absorb from. In Germany, for example, this led us to pick a World Cup soccer match over a Wagner opera, although I must say The Flanker had a strong voice in that decision.

Our first real venture into family-oriented culture was introduced on a narrow country road by a sign that read: STRATFORD UPON AVON.

We hadn't tried to camp near London, but rather had rented a sort of loft-suite on the top of a tiny hotel just off Kensington High Street. Three of us slept on the floor, and what with eating in the hotel about half the time (hot plate and small "fridge"), it hadn't been what you'd call the luxurious London life-style. So in Stratford we pulled a switcheroo and stayed across the street from the Royal Shakespeare Theatre at the Arden Hotel.

The Arden was very clean, fresh-flowered, organdy-curtained—and stuffy, a country cousin to the Royal Clarence of Exeter. The kids had a room for four on a pretty little back patio, and except for using one of their windows to get in and out of the hotel (the management kept locking the back door on us), we all behaved rather well, I thought. But put lodging aside, for in the charming city by the river Avon, "the play's the thing." In this respect, and in view of the wide range of age and interest represented in our little group, we got two breaks right off: The Royal Shakespeare Theatre's production for our day at Stratford would be the comedy "As You Like It," and we could see a matinee. "As You Like It" turned out to be a delightful introduction to Shakespeare for the younger members of the family; and the kids proved twice as alert and receptive in the afternoon, so matinees became a habit throughout our year.

"As You Like It," you will remember, is the story of the beautiful Rosalind, whose father makes his home in the forest of Arden after being banished, his estates evilly appropriated by a wicked brother. Disguised as a boy, Rosalind also goes off into the idyllic woods and is there brilliantly, if briefly, freed from the restraints of womanhood.

At the end (I loved this), when Rosalind decides to reveal her identity and succumb to her true female nature in order to be united with her beloved Orlando, she says with profundity—and a wink—"I will dwindle into a wife." What the Royal Shakespeare Theatre did with this play (and not a hard thing to do with Shakespeare), through background brochures and subtle direction, was to fit it like a glove on the current women's liberation movement.

In the morning before attending the play, we had all read together the synopsis of "As You Like It" and learned that in Shakespeare's time women were so unliberated that they were not even allowed on stage and men (or boys) played the female roles. A simple change of costume, however, had at least allowed the poet to liberate Rosalind's mind and wit—if only for a moment.

The kids loved this exquisite production; even Holly hung on every word. There was not a fidget in the Royal Shakespeare Theatre. But it did get *us* started again—feuding over a problem that had been with us since departing the *Queen*.

Holly has a favorite expression which she applies whenever she feels a male associate is doing her in: "Haven't you heard of the women's lib story?" Following the play, with no less a figure than Will Shakespeare to back her up, Holly told the boys: "NOW you've seen the women's lib story. When a girl pretends to be a boy and no one knows the difference, she can do everything and do it better!"

However, before Shakespeare got into the act, the running debate over our male-female roles had not been exactly on a lofty plane. Who would do what in the gypsy life ahead of us? Not knowing exactly what we would face during our year of camping, all I could be sure of at the outset was that there would be an abundance of household tasks every day, and I had hardly known Johnny to make a cup of coffee or wash a dish. What would *he* do? It was my proposal that since all of our chores would be essentially domestic, we should share them. It would be a fantastic opportunity for the boys to learn to cook, because camp cooking is a hell of a lot more fun than home cooking (at least that was my pitch). And it wouldn't hurt them to wash a dish now and then either.

But before we ever had a chance to try my idea in practice, Johnny rebelled in theory. The boys, he said, would not, repeat WOULD NOT cook and do dishes. We had one royal verbal battle—

but when it came right down to it, what was I going to do? I question what Betty Friedan and Gloria Steinem would have done in the same situation, locked as I was into a 6-by-13-foot box with a former All-Pro.

So, although the girls and I sulked off and on for a while, all of us settled into the most traditional of roles. However, as it worked out, these were not 20th century roles, but traditional roles of the 19th, 18th, 17th centuries—which included domestic chores for the men. For example, I couldn't take my shopping list to the supermarket for the week's supplies because we saw no more than a half-dozen such phenomena during the entire year. Johnny didn't plant and harvest the crops, but he hunted, scrounged, and bargained for our food. At home, I pay all the bills, a task he finds tedious, depressing, and time-consuming. On the road, with his quantitative mind (my mind's qualitative, I maintain), he handled the constant problem of currency exchange and fielded the potential rippers-off. And during inclement weather he sometimes hiked miles around to find us clean, low-cost shelter. I did the hand wash, but whenever possible, he would take a huge bundle of laundry on his back and search for a launderette or a reasonably priced laundry.

That's the way it all worked out—eventually. But at Stratford, still embroiled in this battle of the sexes, we were all—that is, we girls were all—thrilled to see how the Bard had handled it back in the 1500s.

The kids wanted to stay in Stratford two more days because "Hamlet" was coming up in the theatre company's revolving schedule. But we had a deadline to meet—our only deadline of the year. We had to be at the Soviet border near Helsinki, Finland, on October 1, and we wanted to see some of Scandinavia first. Besides, we thought, they adore Shakespeare now and have experienced his genius, and "Hamlet" might be too much too soon for the younger children.

In the week following our visit to Stratford, Dan and Debbie re-read and studied "As You Like It," as well as all the material we could find on the life of Shakespeare. It was a case of planting good seeds of learning by making the right choices from what a certain culture had to offer.

However, I must say Deb and Holly and I were destined to end the visit to William Shakespeare's hometown in a downright funk.

Leaving the Arden Hotel, the boys carried the first wave of luggage out to the van. Without our knowledge and with The Dad contributing a grain of historical irony ("Martin Luther liked to nail signs on church doors"), Dan taped to the door of the Beast the following quote from the Royal Shakespeare Theatre's brochure:

> Men have broad shoulders and narrow hips and accordingly they possess intelligence. Women have narrow shoulders and broad hips. Women ought to stay at home; the way they were created indicates this, for they have broad hips and a wide fundament to sit upon, keep house and bear and raise children. [Luther 1531]

And they say women always have the last word?

We gave up using campgrounds in England; they were overcrowded in late August. Johnny called them "crampgrounds." However, we found that, as long as you asked first, there was no problem in camping on private property. Which led to an interesting though unsettling experience.

It was sunset when we finally turned off the road and got permission from a farmer to camp on his property. He'd said, "Of course, any place on my land," but suggested the deserted World War II airstrip because there we wouldn't get stuck in the mud.

Most nights we looked for a sheltered place to park the camper. Well, that's not altogether true. *Tim* looked for a sheltered place for the porta-pot. Johnny always preferred a high spot, "something with a view," and had, on occasion, taken us way past dark looking for a place with a view. I couldn't have cared less. I just wanted to get the spaghetti cooking.

You know, it's eerie, and I mean downright eerie, when *two* people get that I've-lived-through-this-before feeling at the same instant. But the minute we'd passed the tangle of ripe blackberries and bumped onto the old concrete apron, Johnny and I were struck by this sensation simultaneously.

You couldn't even see the airstrip until you were on it, but there it was: Forten Heath Air Force Base, near the village of Shrewsbury, smack-dab in the middle of England. It was dusk and a gentle breeze was coming up. There was absolute quiet . . . Then both of us, in our minds' eyes, saw a balding Dean Jagger wheeling his bicycle through the weeds, scanning the sky for incoming B-17s . . . and we knew we'd been to Forten Heath before—in the movies. The film of which this remote, quiet spot was so evocative was "Twelve O'Clock High."

Taken with the spirit of the place, Johnny gunned the engines (er, engine), and we sped half a mile down a cracked runway to the middle of the old base. There was a small, thick stand of trees bursting through the concrete. "Stop!" screamed Tim. And so we placed our potty at just about the point the bombers would have lifted off.

Being old movie fans, Johnny and I tried to recall—occasionally playing trivia back and forth—all the details of "Twelve O'Clock High."

"What was the big mission?"

"Daylight bombing."

"So what?"

"It was the first time in World War II."

"Right. Why was it important?"

"Ball bearings . . . all Hitler's war machines needed ball bearings."

"Of course," mused Dan.

"Name the three targets."

"Schweinhaven . . . something . . . and Peenemünde."

"No, dummy, Peenemünde was where the Germans were working on the V-2—that was another movie."

While I mixed a couple of cocktails and our small home became a kitchen-family room, Johnny and I began to reconstruct for the kids the way it might have been 30 years ago right here in this desolate, lonely spot.

We told how the movie described Gregory Peck's catatonic crack-up when so few of his bomber pilots returned to England (by this time our minds were made up: "Twelve O'Clock High" was set at Forten Heath *for sure!*) . . . which led us to a discussion of battle fatigue. Were they American pilots? From there we got into the R.A.F. and the Battle of Britain and British bravery and stoicism and Churchill. The lights of the Beast burned alone on that runway until midnight as we conjured from memory the images of World War II.

We rolled out of our sleeping bags soon after sunup, and after breakfast jogged to the other end of what by now we had code-named "runway Baker." We peeked into Forten Heath's lone remaining Quonset hut and saw two pigs and a plow. Then we all ran back to the Beast and climbed in. Johnny, still absorbed in the war, taxied, not toward the road which would take us to the highway and north to England's Lake District, but off through the weeds and saplings to the far end of the main runway. There he turned slowly, put the Blue Bomber in neutral, revved up the engine, and checked us out.

"Jeannie! Windows shut?"

"Check!"

"Tim! Battery charged?"

"Check!"

"Holly! Fuel OK?"

"Fuel?"

"Gasoline."

"Check!"

"Deb! Seat belts fastened?"

"Dad . . . what are you DOING?"

"Off we go, into the wild blue yonder, climbing high into the sky!" sang Johnny. And he gassed it! Oh boy, did he gas it!

"This is no goddamn Ferrari!" I yelled.

"Right, it's a B-17," Dan shot back, laughing, loving the speed.

"Thirty . . . forty . . . fifty," Johnny shouted.

"Watch the tree, Dad!"

"How long are these runways?"

"At least two miles."

"Sixty . . . "

"THIS IS A TRUCK, FOR GODSAKE!"

Deb screamed, Holly cried, I prayed, Dan laughed, Tim held on, and Johnny . . . finally slowed down. It was some kind of ride; we burst through the brambles and back onto the road. It had been some kind of "flight"—a strange 12 hours.

Behind us, Dean Jagger climbed onto his bicycle and pedaled off into the sunrise.

The Helsinki Warning

Now that the trip has ended, it's safe to talk about the weather. By September 11, when we made our Scandinavian landfall in Stavanger, Norway, talking about the weather had become a no-no. The weather had been almost ideal throughout Ireland and England, and we felt much like a pitcher in the sixth inning of a no-hitter: Mention our incredible luck, and it might change. You may not believe this, but only once during the year did weather alter our plans, and that was when we were praying for a snowstorm—and got only rain.

The Dad, with his tendency toward seasickness, had a genuine apprehension about the North Sea crossing from Newcastle-upon-Tyne, England, to Bergen, Norway, which was our eventual destination. But the sea was very gentle, the sky overcast, the temperature

47

just above cool. When the ferryboat *Jupiter* chugged into Stavanger for a one-hour layover, Johnny took the kids ashore for a look at the ancient seaport, and I remained aboard to catch up on the mail. Moments after the five of them left our cabin, I saw the sun break through the clouds; and the picturesque harbor, which had been cast in black and white, was suddenly radiant with color. "They must have just stepped ashore," I thought. That's the way our luck with the weather was going.

And the luck stayed with us through Scandinavia as we headed the Beast east to our appointed date with the Russians on October 1. Had it not been for that deadline, we would have lingered many places in Norway, Sweden, and Finland, immersed in the most magnificent fall we had ever seen.

Where would we have lingered? Bergen, deep in the throat of a fjord, spectacular, charming, with its vibrant dockside market selling everything from live fish to what seemed like a trillion magnificent flowers; Geilo, in winter a famous Norwegian ski resort but in September warm and nearly deserted (and inexpensive); Oslo, a great city, where we went to a *salg* (sale) and for $159 (our biggest single expenditure so far) bought six pairs of boots, five ski jackets, and an almost matched set of "workout" shirts. This turned out to be a super purchase; Norwegian sportswear, especially winter sportswear, can't be beaten for lightness, durability, and warmth. However, finding any kind of a bargain in Scandinavia is unusual.

Actually, the prices we paid during our trip aren't even worth remembering. The inflation rates of the countries we visited ranged between 12 percent and 30 percent during a year when, with prices already on the rise, the Arabs added the oil embargo to the confused state of the world's interlocking economies. But even taking that into consideration, I must tell you that any way you do it, it's relatively expensive to put yourself in a position to view the beauties of Scandinavia. After an $80 day in Bergen (and at that our "hotel" was the dormitory of a closed bible school), we tried to beat the costs by following the *hytter* trail.

Perhaps because of the increasing costs of travel, Norway alone has over 500 new campgrounds, and each of these contains *hytter,* little cabins that rent, or did, for $8 a night. Each *hytte,* or cabin, has electric heat, four plank bunks (bring your own sleeping bag), a table and benches, and a hot plate for cooking. The campgrounds are wonderfully clean. The bathrooms smell of disinfectant, and the cabins smell of the fresh timber from which they are built. I liked that. We put the kids in the *hytte,* and Johnny and I stayed in the Beast. The van was an altogether different place when used as a master bedroom rather than a dorm.

Unfortunately (according to Tim and Holly), a *hytte* also made an excellent one-room schoolhouse; and so Johnny declared the fall term officially open and began tutoring the younger kids. In the interest of complete accuracy, I must tell you that Dan instructed Tim in mathematics. Johnny found fifth grade "new math" too difficult to master. ("Ridiculous," he grumbled.)

Although Sweden had cabins too, there we took an even more interesting course. The Swedes (which seems consistent with their profile) have a free camping rule. So long as you observe certain rules about litter and sanitation, you can pitch camp anywhere out of sight of a farmhouse or other inhabited building.

That's how we found Ake Piehl. We were tooling along toward Stockholm, driving downhill, or so it seemed, ever since "peaking" our last pass in Norway, when a natural phenomenon occurred earlier than we had expected. It got dark. So, knowing the Swedish camping rule, we turned off the main road into some woods and started driving around dirt roads looking for a fairly sheltered place. That's when we almost literally ran into Ake. He invited us to camp well within sight of his structure. In fact, we slept in his farmyard. Ake had lived in the United States years before and said he would be in the States yet, except for a heart problem. Medical and disability benefits in socialized Sweden made it much more practical for Ake to return to the family farm. Still, he had a brother living in the United States, near Chicago. It turned out that Ake Piehl's brother lived about ten miles from our home in Palatine, Illinois.

That night at Ake's, in order to relieve the congestion in the Beast, we initiated a new sleeping policy. Johnny and I bedded down outside on the ground. It was windy and growing cold, so we put on our Chicago Bear stocking caps, stuck our sleeping bags into great plastic garbage bags—and slumbered like babies. Ake thought we were nuts. We awoke at 5:00 A.M. to find him laughing over us. He was on his way out to feed the pigs.

We'd read in the *International Herald Tribune* that Sweden's respected and beloved King Gustaf VI Adolf had died at age 91 after a productive and exemplary life. We arrived in Stockholm in time for his funeral. Sweden had seen a great deal of political turmoil in the past few months, a critical election was coming up, and the new king, Gustaf's grandson, Carl Gustaf, would no longer have what few monarchical powers had been left to his grandfather.

With weeping thousands we watched the solemn funeral procession: a horse-drawn black casket, followed on foot by the young King Carl, the major figures of Sweden's government, and representatives from around the world. We had a profound sense of participating in the history of this small but admirable nation.

For us, despite the sadness of the occasion, there was one note of amusement. We just had to chuckle at the Swedish National Guard, which is the country's military organization—and I use that term loosely. The young soldiers lined the streets in rumpled uniforms that must have been dug out of trunks all over the land, their long, usually blond locks trailing from misperched caps, guns held every which way. The detachments of soldiers in the parade didn't appear to have the vaguest idea of how to march. We ran into a Dane whom we'd met at our campground. "You think the Swedes are bad," he chortled. "You should see *our* army!" We didn't think the Swedes were bad; we thought it was kind of a nice army.

Somebody in our gang came up with a brilliant idea in Stockholm. It was actually suggested that we check *in advance* on the ferry crossing the Baltic to Finland. It would have taken a week to drive around that great, gray sea. We found that by ferrying to Turku, Finland, we could see at least a little of that country on the way to Helsinki.

Ferryboats are a bargain in Europe, but only in the sense that in most places it costs less to go across than around. They certainly offer little in the way of sightseeing opportunities. We took eleven ferry trips altogether during our year—and only the two shortest were in daylight. The ferryboats all run at night. The classic example is the ferry plying the Adriatic from Dubrovnik, Yugoslavia, to Bari, Italy: The distance is about 150 miles, and the boats leave at midnight and arrive at 7:00 A.M. A customs official told us that nighttime operation was mainly an accommodation to commercial traffic—truckers found it more convenient to drive onto the ferry at night and sleep, then get up and drive off next morning to reach their destinations during working hours. We thought there must be more to it than that, and finally figured it out this way: Since the ships had to be a certain (large) size to handle the seas we crossed (the Irish, the North, the Baltic, the Mediterranean, and so on), the ferry operators wanted to utilize the full capacity of their ships while at the same time maximizing their profits. The ferryboats generally carried from one and a half to two levels of vehicles, above which were a couple of decks of cabins, and above the cabins were bars and restaurants. Night travel discouraged touristry nonsense like spreading a picnic lunch on deck to enjoy the scenery and sunlight of a daytime cruise and allowed them to sell you dinner, breakfast, and a cabin, or at least a chair, to sleep in. Besides, they needed to carry few crew members to serve sleeping passengers.

But it took us a while to figure all this out, so we went for the "con" on the Baltic route and rented two cabins. It was a waste of money. Nobody slept because it was our first rough sea. Johnny finally got to tell me, "I told you so. Seasickness is not all in my head." He threw up all night, poor baby. The rest of us were fine.

A couple of days later in a campground outside Helsinki, we woke up, pulled back the curtains of the Beast, and what to our wondering eyes did appear—SNOW! It was just a flurry, and the sun soon broke through; but it was our first flurry, and we kept thinking of that freezing movie "Dr. Zhivago." In four days we would be in Russia. We knew the driving would be difficult enough in the Soviet Union without bad weather. We were beginning to tense up.

Moving from west to east we got a sort of color profile of Scandinavia. Norway had been almost gay, the people strode rather than strolled; Sweden, also bright but, we thought, a little more subdued than Norway; Finland was less colorful still. The Finns dressed more in browns, grays, and blacks. The standard of cleanliness, the quality of goods, and the friendliness of the people remained consistently high in all three countries.

One of the first things I noticed upon entering Helsinki was the street signs. Most were printed in Finnish and Swedish. When there was a third or even a fourth language, English and German followed in that order. Little Finland's neighbor to the east was the biggest nation in the world in land area, one of the globe's two superstates, *and* a powerful influence in Finland's affairs; yet the Russian language was apparently not needed in Helsinki. For Russia, Finland is a source, for example, of furniture, electronic products, and many of the consumer goods available to the privileged in the Soviet Union. Although reportedly there are numerous Soviet government functionaries living in Finland, there aren't many Russian tourists there. The few Russians who do come are on carefully guided and approved tours; so the signs are printed for the rest of us.

We didn't properly see Helsinki, because even if there was no Cyrillic lettering on the signs, the Big Bear to the east loomed large in our minds. In addition to stocking up on food, we went to the American Consulate on Helsinki's quiet Embassy Row to make a final check on what we should expect upon crossing the Soviet border.

And—POW!—we got it, right between the eyes, in the form of a printed circular issued by the U.S. State Department and spoken admonitions delivered by a member of the consular staff. Its rather ominous tone prompted us to refer thereafter to the advice we received as "The Helsinki Warning."

The press at the time was daily carrying reports on the Andrei Sakharov-Alexander Solzhenitsyn "dialogues" with the Soviet government. Also, Richard Nixon and Henry Kissinger were well into their détente policies. Henry ("Scoop") Jackson was adding his cautionary voice to the American debate regarding concessions to the Russians. We didn't know it, but the Yom Kippur War in the Middle East and the resultant oil embargo were about to burst upon the international scene. We were carefully following all of these events (as part of the children's lessons) in the English-language publications available to us, principally the *International Herald Tribune,* printed in Paris, and the European editions of *Time* and *Newsweek.* It could have been the best of times or the worst of times to enter the Soviet Union. We didn't know.

The Helsinki Warning was issued on the assumption that *any* time could be the worst of times. Our own subsequent observations of the Soviet security and propaganda systems, both of which can be tightened or relaxed by the Kremlin at will, confirmed that this was a reasonable assumption. We entered Russia at perhaps the best of times because, as we saw again and again during our travel there, the Soviets need American trade and technology *badly,* and they were not about to let such internal questions as Jewish emigration policy, discontented intellectuals, or external wars and embargoes stand in the way of Russia's immediate requirements or Communism's ultimate aim. Despite the warmth and friendliness of the ordinary Russian citizen, we didn't see or read anything in the Soviet Union (*or* in Europe, *or* in the United States) that would belie a statement made by Vladimir Ilich Lenin over a half-century before: "When it comes time to hang the capitalists, they will hand us the rope to do it with."

The man we spoke to at the consulate in Helsinki told us that, to his knowledge, no Americans had entered Russia by automobile from Finland since the previous June. He said to keep a low profile, to obey all the traffic regulations (which, so far as he knew, were not printed anywhere in English), to be careful about taking pictures, and to see that each of the kids committed to memory the telephone number of the American Embassy in Moscow. We were warned that almost any printed matter might be confiscated as well as any valuables not declared upon entry. The man shook his head a lot—especially when he escorted us out and spied the kids and the Beast. As we drove out onto the shaded street, he waved and wished us luck.

Helsinki was a nervous place.

Stuck in a ditch . . . in Connemara.

Our neighbors,
the cows.

First and second
place in the 100
meters — different
heats, of course.

When you're camping,
sometimes a cold stream
is more private
(and more beautiful)
than a hot shower.

Forten Heath Air Force Base. We'd been there in the movies.

Had we more time in Scandinavia we could have . . .

shopped daily in the Bergen market . . .

fished again in the fjord.

Red Square inspired awe in us . . .

the Beast inspired awe in them.

The changing of the guard at Lenin's tomb.

For our last 1,000 miles in the U.S.S.R., Johnny had to drive with his infected foot elevated. This is my normal driving posture.

Beginning in Russia, Holly became Johnny's constant companion at borders, hotels, markets—anyplace an advantage would be . . . advantageous.

2,600 Miles of Red Tape

We were the only clients for the Soviet border guards as the military jeep that had been following us for the past two miles passed us and pulled ahead to a stop, indicating that now we were in the hands of customs officials. One of the four look-alike young uniformed officials stepped forward and demanded our passports while his three companions stood staring with open admiration at our Ford camper.

We were all somewhat tense, Johnny especially so since it was he who held the documents and would deal with the problems we'd been told we were almost sure to encounter at the Soviet border. With his new beard giving him a hip aura, Johnny had found that having little Holly beside him in every foray into the unknown precincts of border stations, hotel desks, and tourist offices was a distinct advantage. She was next to him today, in the "porto" position (i.e., sitting on the covered porta-pot which, wedged between two bucket seats, gave us room for three in front). Holly was smiling (as instructed), not really understanding what was going on. "I didn't know the Russians spoke a different alphabet," she said, as Dan tried to explain the Cyrillic lettering on the border tower and why C.C.C.P. meant U.S.S.R., which meant Russia, "sort of." "Be quiet," Johnny muttered unnecessarily as we waited for the soldier to return.

The "No Cameras" signs had begun to appear several hundred yards before the Finnish (no pun) line as we approached the border earlier that afternoon. Next we had noted the trash cans placed about every 50 yards along our route. Taking the hint, Johnny stopped while I sadly deposited my paperback copy of Solzhenitsyn's *The First Circle* in the last bin. I felt even worse later when I learned that the cans were primarily for the pornography prized by Russian truck drivers who were lucky enough to draw the Helsinki run.

From the time a kindly Finn guard had lifted the gate to let us pass through a no-man's-land extending perhaps 100 yards—and out of the so-called free world—we had encountered no less than five Soviet checkpoints, four actual gates.

Now, on a bright fall afternoon, the six of us sat waiting beside the sparkling stone-and-glass Soviet customs building, set on a slight knoll in an almost deserted countryside. Facing the building, across six lanes of pavement, was a 200-foot tower emblazoned with the letters "C.C.C.P." The tower was crowned with antennas and other communications paraphernalia. And above all of this, a huge, red banner—now floating, now flapping—winked its hammer and sickle at the anxious Americans below.

Dan was literally aching to take a picture.

For me, being in that place at that time was such a dream come true that I could not believe it was happening. A few months earlier at a dinner in Washington, D.C., no less a personage than NBC's capital bureau chief, a man who had traveled extensively throughout the world, had told us that we would not be allowed to drive through Russia, that what we planned was impossible. A lot of Red tape had been involved, including the requirement that we submit personal biographies to Intourist, Russia's state travel agency. And we'd had to schedule our arrival in Russia to conform to the date "suggested" by our Intourist representative. Nevertheless, we'd had to knock down no real barriers in order to obtain the necessary clearances.

We entered Russia with a kind of non-background that lent spirit to our adventure. We had purposely read no guidebooks, no "advice" written by previous visitors. Nor had we arranged ahead for any of the special tours and treatment Intourist offers to foreign "opinion makers" as well as others whom they deem worthy of what amounts to a public-relations effort. We had a friend who had a friend who'd driven in Russia and we'd thought about calling him to see what to expect, but changed our minds. We wanted to be surprised. We were.

What seriously worried us after The Helsinki Warning was the fact that we were carrying our whole year's household in the van, and the rules explicitly stated that authorities would only permit what one needed for the length of his visit—in our case, two weeks—in the U.S.S.R. For example, Intourist said that each person was allowed one "amateur cine-camera" with one set of accessories. We had two professional still cameras (and about 2,000 shots of film), one news-film camera, 5,000 feet of 16 mm. film, and two tape recorders with 50 blank cassettes. And that's not all we had.

As we waited there at the customs station, our pre-search tension mounting, Deb finally cracked and revealed to us the hitherto-unsuspected presence of "Gert-rude." Gert-rude (you'll have to take my word for it) was a 12-pound rock. Just a dumb gray rock that Debbie had picked up in Lake Geneva, Wisconsin, during a school outing. Gert hadn't even got any sparkly stuff in her. Believe me, she was a dud.

But Debbie isn't. Despite her grubby jeans, she really has all the instincts of that supposedly passé creature we used to call "a lady." The great thrust of kindness implicit in this description Debbie lavishes on what Dan refers to as her "critter friends," in whom she discerns remarkable and individual characteristics. I call her insight "imagina-tion." Over the years, Deb has written and illustrated fairy tale after adventurous fairy tale about a tiny critter called "Macti." I always empathized happily with Macti. But not Gert-rude. Rocks leave me cold.

It is only fair to confess that later on we all came to regard Gert with some affection, so often did Deb describe Gert's ambition "to see the real Lake Geneva, in Switzerland." It developed, of course, that the Wisconsin lake is, after all, the "real" Lake Geneva while Geneva, Switzerland's is Lac Léman. In any event, Johnny suggested that Gert-rude might like to die there. But at the moment, as we sat at the Soviet border with God knew what ahead of us, Gert seemed a needless embarrassment. Deb had had the sense not to tell us that her rock was along until we pulled into the customs station. Had she mentioned it earlier, Gert-rude would have died in Helsinki.

We'd been waiting in the car a long ten minutes when a guard finally beckoned us inside the customs building.

"Declare all valuables," the official admonished (mostly in sign language) after Johnny had given only a rough accounting of the cash and traveler's checks he had on hand. So, of course, Holly piped up, "Should I bring my pennies?" "What pennies?" Johnny asked. The contents of her piggy bank, she said. It was all in a plastic bag and she would get it. I about croaked when Holly dumped the plastic bag out on the counter, where a smiling guard started to help her. She and her soldier friend, heads together and concentrating on the job at hand, counted out almost $30 in small change and dollar bills.

Since no other travelers had yet appeared at the station, our parade was the center of attention. Not a few of the Russians looked disgusted, some amused, when we emptied the Beast of our luggage— 16 pieces as it turned out, all sizes, shapes, and colors. Certainly no one treated this spectacle as an everyday occurrence. I couldn't figure out how to disappear. "A year we gotta live on this stuff, a year," Johnny kept repeating. But after looking at a tenth pair of Levi's even a Russian has got to be bored. The van was what concerned us, and the kids and I watched anxiously from inside as, per instruction, two guards flanked The Flanker and went out to inspect the Beast.

Neither the spare car parts (so valuable in Russia's black market) nor the film seemed to faze the guards as they probed, even using mirrors, throughout the camper. Gert was buried deep and never surfaced.

The guards worried over the binoculars, thumbed through Dan's Motocross magazines, and ignored *Time* and *Newsweek* as well as George Orwell's indictment of their system, *Animal Farm*. They punched up the tape recorder to listen to one of Deb's favorite "critter" friends, a Beatle, singing "Back in the U.S.S.R." Deb had deliberately programmed the tape to what she considered a diplomatic choice of songs. But the guards didn't understand English. Neither did they seem to recognize the "depraved" Beatles, though they seemed to enjoy the music.

We later concluded that the search—indeed, our whole two-hour exposure at customs—might well have been something of a charade, that we had been cleared in advance. Détente seemed to be in the air as well as in the news.

The customs officials instructed us to report directly to Intourist at the central railroad station in Vyborg, where we would be informed of our itinerary for the next two weeks and our lodging for the night—in Leningrad. Johnny looked on the map and said, "Leningrad's only 120 miles, like New York to Boston. No sweat." It was the last such comparison he ever made. Driving in the Soviet Union is not like driving anywhere in the United States. The U.S. State Department warning read:

> Automobile travel along certain specified routes is permitted, with or without Intourist guides. Only mature and experienced drivers should consider unaccompanied motor trips. Driving conditions are far more rugged than in Western Europe; service stations are rare. Soviet driving regulations are complex and very strictly enforced. Foreign drivers who violate them are subject to the full severity of the law (including trial and imprisonment).

It was 5:30 P.M. before we left the border scene and we hadn't eaten since breakfast, so when we reached Vyborg about two hours later, Deb and I started dinner. I say *started*.

We had groped our way through the darkened streets looking for the railroad station. There were street lights in Vyborg, but few were turned on. Although the 1973–74 "energy crisis" had only been hinted at before we got beyond range of the Western press, we found the Russians long accustomed to conserving heat and light, a practice that added to the general dullness of the surroundings. Later, of course, we were to see the same measures taken all over Western Europe, at least temporarily.

What was markedly visible as we approached the hulking silhouette of the massive old terminal was a series of bright bulbs etching the number "1917." "We really *are* here," I said. "Nineteen seventeen. The year of the Great Bolshevik Revolution . . . the October Revolution. And today's October first—an omen!"

Just then the bulbs blinked and the number changed. "Mother," Tim said, squelching what he knew to be the beginning of an historical dissertation. "It's a clock, just like on the Palatine National Bank." Tim was right, and translated from "European time," "1918" meant that it was 7:18 P.M. But it was still October 1, even though we felt like a week had passed since leaving Helsinki that morning. And I had to do something about getting food into the family.

We parked the Beast in the square, about 100 yards from the terminal. Johnny and Holly went in, Dan got behind the wheel, and Tim was poised to run for Dad if we encountered any trouble. Deb and I switched on the interior lights and began to pull food out of the refrigerator to prepare a little meal. We were famished.

The next thing we knew, we were no longer the Morris clan fixing a routine meal as we'd done nearly every day during six weeks of camping throughout Great Britain and Scandinavia. We were monkeys in a zoo. The people (all men) who had been scattered across the square were now drawn to the van as if to a magnet. And although we were the monkeys, they were doing all the chattering, noses pressed against the windows, staring inside.

It was at that moment we first felt how very foreign we were. Everything seemed to astound them, from the cherry-red tomatoes and green lettuce I was cutting to the bright Norwegian ski jackets we were wearing to the gleaming coppertone refrigerator and efficient stainless steel-topped stove. Eventually we got used to this staring, which wasn't unfriendly at all and indeed offered many opportunities for making friends with Russian people. But on this night, hungry as we were, Deb and I could not put up with it. So we switched off the lights and huddled down in the van to stare back at the people who would be our hosts for the next two weeks.

Johnny and Holly were gone for a half-hour, disappearing almost into another time frame, so 1940-ish was the scene. Soldiers were everywhere, most in dun-colored, calf-length trench coats. I kept expecting Humphrey Bogart to skulk by.

When Johnny returned with a big envelope full of documents, he quickly appropriated my black vinyl carrying case, which we just as quickly dubbed "Dad's purse." Intourist had been expecting us, of course. Throughout our sojourn in Russia we found that we never had to worry about the local Intourist agent leaving his desk before we checked in, despite the lateness of the hour. They didn't go off alert until all their charges were bedded down, passports turned in at assigned hotels.

We had been directed to the Hotel Leningrad and given an envelope containing meal coupons for three squares a day for 14 days for six people, all pre-purchased months before from an Intourist representative in Chicago. "At least we won't go hungry," Johnny laughed. Wrong again, Flanker.

There was only one road from Vyborg to Leningrad, so we didn't have to worry about getting lost. As soon as we left the city, I switched the light back on and tried again to fix a meal. At the risk of horrifying Ralph Nader and his safety sleuths, I must say that maintaining your balance while standing in a moving vehicle is fantastic for the legs. I had to do it constantly in Russia, so demanding was our itinerary. By the end of our visit, I had the muscle tone of a 20-year-old. Of course, you need an extraordinarily lousy road to work with, but in Russia that's "standard equipment."

I cannot describe how dark and lonely that road to Leningrad was. On the infrequent occasions when we did encounter another vehicle (usually a truck equipped with low running lights), it would invariably set up a furious honking and blinking. From this we soon deduced (correctly, it turned out) that headlights were banned on Soviet highways. Finally, unable to beat them, Johnny joined them. He switched off the headlights.

The Flanker chose to mind the rules just as we entered a deep woods. The trees, blowing in the nighttime breeze, were snatching at the small space allowed to the road. We could almost see tiny critter-eyes glowing in the black thickets. I had just stabilized two plates of food on a non-slippery rubber mat and was beginning to slice the bread when Johnny let out an ungodly scream, jammed on the brakes, and jerked the wheel. The knife I was holding flew off harmlessly while I slammed to the floor. Deb fell on top of me. Tim, who was on a back bench, was thrown into the counter with a crunch. In the front, Holly somehow ducked softly under the padded dash, while

Johnny simply hung on and cussed. "We've just hit a moose," he finally managed to say. There was a long moment when I knew, just *knew,* the trip was over, that if we didn't die, it was the K.G.B. for sure.

Johnny said the moose was 7 feet tall, and Holly agreed. None of the rest of us saw it. Since he was operating in the dark (literally), Johnny hadn't spotted the moose standing in the middle of the road until we were almost upon it . . . at which point the beast had tried to outrace the Beast, heading right across our path toward the forest.

"Press on, press on," Deb was saying almost immediately in her best hoity-toity accent. Animal lover that she is, Debbie was content when Johnny said the moose had galloped, not limped, into the woods. But The Flanker wasn't about to press on. With all of us begging him not to, he pulled over to the trees and got out to inspect the damage. We were exhausted, and surely more frightened than we should have been (I like to think), but we'd had enough of men in uniform for one day; it would be just our luck now to have a convoy drive by.

When it began to seem like Johnny had been fiddling around the headlight forever, I went out to check on him. And there was The Flanker, flashlight in hand, calmly picking moose hairs out of the Beast's chromium trappings. "Getting rid of the evidence," he said. There was a healthy dent above the light. Praying the moose was less damaged, we climbed back in the van. Although it wasn't in the Helsinki Warning, surely there had to be a Soviet law against murdering a moose.

When we awakened on October 2, it was as if from a dream . . . or perhaps we had just slid from one dream to another. The view from our room on the seventh floor of the Hotel Leningrad was magnificent. I was more than content just to stare out the window and cogitate on this first morning in the Soviet Union.

The children were exhausted from the previous day, so they decided to rest and write letters to their good and loyal friends back home, telling the story of "the day we crossed the border." Our youngest has a talent for economy in composition which, combined with her lousy spelling, may someday qualify her as a great television news writer. She allowed me to copy her note to her dear friend, Ann Mayer, who lives across the street from us.

DEAR ANNIE:

The first day in Russia after we got surched, we were driving at night and I was in frunt and my Mom was cutting bread. All of the sudden my dad honked, yeld, swirved, and put on his brakes. So my mom droped the knife and sat on the floor and we hit a MOOSE ! ! !
tim got a broos
nothing serios

Love,
HOLLY

The tempo of our trip through the U.S.S.R. reminded me of a piece humorist Art Buchwald once did on breaking the record for the "five-minute Louvre." The deadlines were back-breaking. We did all the sightseeing and cultural things Intourist planned for us. The Hermitage Museum in Leningrad alone was worth the trip. The Kremlin was awe- and fear-inspiring. So was the embalmed body of Lenin in Red Square. So, in fact, was Red Square.

But those sightseeing excursions were minimal in their impact when compared with the time- and energy-consuming business of "living" while touring the Soviet Union.

Believe me, Intourist is a tyrant unto itself. On arrival in each city we were required to check in at the agency's local office. This procedure, although it is nicely designed to keep tabs on the traveler, consumed hours of time over the course of our visit. The address of each Intourist office is available in the official guide—and it is very thoughtfully written in Western alphabet. But the street signs are in Cyrillic. The situation is not impossible; it's just damn irritating.

Intourist boasts that foreign tourists can now visit over a hundred Soviet cities—which is pretty exciting compared to the restrictions in, say, 1937 or even 1957. Yet at least a quarter of Russia is absolutely and officially closed, and Intourist will not make arrangements for travel to most of the Soviet Union, in effect closing much of the balance of this land, which comprises about one-sixth of the earth's dry surface and holds 248 million people. It takes 2,000 miles of driving due east in Russia just to get to some real mountains, the Urals. You can take the train to Vladivostok on the Pacific Coast, which the Russians claim is "the world's biggest travel bargain," but you can only get off at certain specified stops to look around. We didn't travel by train in the hinterlands, but we talked to people who did. The consensus was that it was cheap all right—and you got what you paid for.

On Friday, after four days in Leningrad, we started the next leg of our journey. As we drove into the flat countryside en route to Novgorod and Moscow, we hoped to see something of how the Russian people lived, but the by now well-worn Helsinki Warning cautioned:

> Any marked deviation from a scheduled itinerary will draw immediate and strong reaction from Soviet Authorities. A law of July 23, 1966, provides penalties for foreigners who "maliciously" violate Soviet travel regulations: "Visiting places not mentioned in their U.S.S.R. entry visas or deviating from the itinerary indicated in the travel documents without special permission." Soviet policemen have the right to assess fines for violation of these rules without recourse to local authorities. If a foreigner has been twice subject to an "administrative penalty" for unauthorized deviations, the law provides that the punishment for a third offense may range from a fine of up to 50 rubles ($80) to a sentence of one year in prison or corrective labor camp.

What seems to happen most often in practice, though, is that when a foreigner gets too nosy the Russians simply pack him up and move him out. And we weren't ready to leave. Even if we thought the rules were dumb, we were anxious to obey them. As it turned out, two weeks of just attempting to obey the rules was an adventure within an adventure; mostly because there is no way of knowing what the rules are.

The land we traveled through on our way to Novgorod looked much like America's Midwest. The road, though rough in places and generally with only a single lane in either direction, was straight and often lined with trees leafed out in October gold. Every bit of land was in use. While in some places cabbages still lay in the fields, in others the winter wheat crop was beginning to put a green sheen on the rich, brown earth. There were plenty of horse-drawn implements and wagons. Where there was machinery, it was handled by men, while the women worked the fields with their hoes and hand tools—or sometimes just with their hands.

As a matter of fact, everywhere we went in the U.S.S.R. we saw more women than men. The Soviet Union boasts that it has far more female doctors of medicine than male, that 37 percent of its lawyers are women as are 32 percent of its engineers. I had always thought of these statistics in terms of progress; but it seems necessity was the mother of this situation. There are 19 million more women than men in the Soviet Union. Later, Johnny, at least, did have occasion to deal with a female doctor, but on this day the women we saw were not so loftily engaged.

That afternoon we saw two female work gangs on the highway, repairing potholes; the women looked lined and weary. Along the roadsides, in what we would call the parkway, old people, almost all of them women, tended milk cows. Unlike the younger people, they seemed to notice nothing, including the Blue Beast. Whereas in other parts of Europe we saw people of all ages and both sexes watching the cattle, in Russia it was always the very, very old who seemed to be, literally, put out to pasture.

At a distance from the highway was what the Russians call an Industrial City. It looked brand-new. We would have given anything (except our freedom) to turn off the highway and drive the mile or so to examine it more carefully. There were large, white buildings that might have been apartments and others that looked like factory buildings. How we would have liked to live in *that* city for three days. But in the rule book it is forbidden even to photograph such a place. We realized what a tiny part of the surface we'd been given to scratch.

There was one disturbing phenomenon which we observed in almost every village along the way. From a central well, old women carried double buckets of water on shoulder yokes back to small homes from which sprouted, almost inevitably, a television aerial. Television and lights the villagers had; but apparently no running water, no indoor plumbing. The stacks of logs piled around whole walls of houses indicated that for both warmth and cooking the fuel was wood.

It was dark by the time we checked into our Novgorod hotel, but not dark enough. We could still see the rooms. They weren't clean. In fact, the bathrooms were filthy. It was in Novgorod that the children conceived the hotel rating system they used for the remainder of our trip. "Super" was top grade, then came "OK," then "skuz." Super was far from luxurious; it simply meant clean and with enough towels and hot water. Skuz meant stained, rough, postage stamp-sized towels, and only occasional, if any, hot water. During our visit to Russia we stayed in six hotels—one super (Moscow), two OKs, and three real skuzes. Novgorod was skuz.

At the time I felt perhaps we were judging too harshly; after all, this was our first East European country. But in our subsequent travels through Poland, Czechoslovakia, Hungary, and Yugoslavia, where we also stayed in hotels, none were skuz. Not one, in fact, fell below Russia's "super" rating. Now, I don't think this is because Russians are dirty people or Soviet maids are especially slovenly—although I have read that sloppy work habits and inefficiency pervade and inhibit the Soviet economic system. But it seems to me that the root cause of dirty hotels—as well as many other factors that irritate not only tourists but Russian citizens, too—is the infernal way the Soviet bureaucracy has of putting carts before horses.

The three skuzes were poor imitations of what I'm sure a Russian dialectician would call "bourgeois American motels." I'm no expert, but it looked like the basic building material was prefabricated concrete slab, a type of construction you see much of here in the United States, and which we also saw in progress in Moscow. But in the skuzes the slabs didn't fit together too well. And such things as hardware and window casings were far below Western standards. Dirt, therefore, not only had ready access but got caught in a lot of unnecessary cracks and crevices. "Somebody up there" decided to build a series of "first class" hostels, but *before* first class material or expertise (or any combination thereof) was available.

Something I *can* bring some knowledge to is housekeeping. Time after time, I would see women sweeping down flights of carpeted stairway with straw brooms. Now I ask you, fellow homemakers, should one install a couple of miles of carpeting without also installing a vacuum cleaner? The bathrooms in the skuz hotels were really the sticking point for me. There were drains in the floors and, although I never saw it done, I think a "good" cleaning was simply a matter of lifting the shower head off its hook and hosing down the room. The sinks and bathtubs were badly stained, and there was encrusted dirt in the places you might expect. An all-pervading odor naturally resulted. I was afraid the kids might become ill, so assiduously did they avoid these bathrooms. "Thank God for the porta-pot," Tim kept saying.

And yet the maids had little besides old-fashioned elbow grease to clean with. A month later, while living in the villa we rented in Yugoslavia, I had to keep bathrooms clean myself and began to appreciate the plight of Soviet maids. Yugoslavia's markets don't compare with ours, yet they would make a Russian housewife wide-eyed with disbelief; but even in Yugoslavia the only abrasive cleanser on the market was a can of diatomaceous earth. You could mount Mr. Clean on a White Tornado and it would still be too late to do anything for those Russian skuz bathrooms. Nevertheless, one must realize that to a Russian *any* kind of a room with *any* kind of a private bath is a great luxury.

Modern hotels and motels are to be found in every city in both Eastern and Western Europe. But in all these other European countries, including those under the Soviet umbrella, there are also traditional hotels and lodging houses, and one can choose. In Russia, one is "assigned." Take it from me, when you're on the road in the Soviet Union, locked into a relentless, unalterable itinerary, things like hot baths, cool drinks, and the morning paper begin to enter your mind as visions of heaven.

That night in Novgorod, we wanted to relax in a clean, comfortable place. And we knew of only one. Johnny and I returned to our Beast and pulled some ice out of the refrigerator to have a quiet little cocktail hour before tackling the dining room.

It was in the Soviet Union that we began to treasure our camper. Personally, my only criterion for a car is that it keep running with reasonably little maintenance. I've never understood people who covet and coddle automobiles. We had many warnings about driving in Eastern Europe; some said we were fools to try. Even though we fed it on gasoline with octane lower than that to which it had been accustomed, our Beast never let us down. It is said that in these days of high fuel prices owning an automobile is like being wed to a lush. But despite the prices we paid for fuel throughout Europe ($40 once, for a tankful in Greece) we never minded much; we could economize on *our* food. From engine to fridge to porta-pot, the Beast was transport, home, and on a night like this one in the middle of the Soviet Union, a haven.

I wrote in my diary that night in Novgorod that the food at dinner was good. But it is a mark of Russian cuisine that I cannot remember what I ate. Some in our family will tell you that Russian food was terrible. I disagree with that. I found it bland and uninteresting, though. I know that somewhere, perhaps in Moscow, there are better restaurants than those we were subjected to. But we were stuck with a budget and those meal tickets, which were good only at Intourist establishments.

You wouldn't think that driving between two major cities in the Soviet Union would be a problem. Between Leningrad and Moscow, though, long lines of trucks, horse-drawn vehicles, an occasional wandering animal, and the rough asphalt single-lane road made the going maddeningly slow. But there were few of what Tim called "regular guy" cars. As more consumer goods become available to the Russians, more "regular guys" will no doubt be driving cars; at least in the cities, the streets are wide and ready for more automobiles. However, presuming that people with cars will be free to travel now and then between those cities, someone ought to put in the order for adequate highways right away. But there it is again: carts before horses, before trucks, before automobiles, and all of them before roads. The Russians aren't backward, they just operate in reverse. Before they roll many more Zhigulis and Zaporozhets off the line, someone better remember that those cars are going to require fuel from time to time. Distances are, well, distant—and gas stations few and far, far between.

There are certain invariable sights encountered when driving through the Russian countryside, and these we remarked upon as we drove on Saturday from Novgorod to Moscow. All along the way, people tended the small vegetable gardens that were a part of even the poorest homes. This we considered quite compatible with what we knew about the legendary strength and persistence of Russia's peasantry. But since we had expected modern Russia to be almost uncompromisingly utilitarian, certain spots of color and beauty surprised and delighted us. For example, the shelters at the ubiquitous bus stops, sometimes designed like lean-tos, sometimes like gazebos, were often built of elaborate materials. They were usually quite colorful, and occasionally were tiny artistic triumphs. (Later we noted a similarly pleasing incongruity in the Moscow subways, their stations vaulted with the grandeur and meticulous mosaic craftsmanship of a Byzantine cathedral.) Where the highway intersected country roads—and even in more remote spots—there were often well-tended parklike areas with wooden benches and monuments to the 20 million war dead of the "Great Patriotic War" (World War II). Not at all surprising, on the other hand, were the constant political posters and slogans: striving, square-jawed men and women, tools in hand, marching forward in the name of progress and the people. Like the gazebos, the signs were in bright colors (mostly red), but I think they could have done with fewer exclamation points. The Russians love exclamation points ! ! ! And everywhere we saw the jaw-jutted profile of Lenin with the reassuring one-liner, "Lenin is always with us." (A Soviet joke: "Why are Russian beds so wide?" "Because Lenin is always with us.")

That Saturday, people were gathered at every bus stop, though we saw very few buses. Every now and then someone along the road would stick out his arm and start jerking it frantically up and down—the Russian "thumb." Finally, we gave in to a particularly persistent waver. The minute Johnny stopped, the hitchhiker yanked open the door and jumped in the Beast's front seat, smiling. *"Spasibo"* (thank you), he said. I had moved with some dispatch to the rear of the bus when the door clicked open.

There was a moment of indecision and then Johnny asked, "Moscow?" The fellow looked perplexed. Then Johnny remembered. *"Moskva?"* he said again. *"Nye, nye, nye, nye,"* said the man in the way so many Russians have of saying *nyet. "Pryama,"* and knifing his arm he indicated that he wanted to go straight down the road.

By this time Tim was in back with the rest of us, sitting on the floor, abandoning the porto, ordinarily a coveted seat. "Wait a minute," he said, "and you'll see why I moved." Sure enough, the man's "perfume" wafted back as we started up.

I was reminded of Henry Luce's observations after a 12-day visit to Russia in 1932, including a harrowing trip on the trans-Siberian railroad. A "czar" of sorts himself in the *Time-Life-Fortune* publishing empire, Luce had no use for the Soviet people or their Communist system, and his only trip there reinforced his prejudice. The editors of *Fortune* had recently printed a comprehensive piece on the Soviet Union that Luce thought was excellent—if not perfect: "The most important specific fact which *Fortune's* story omitted was that the

Russians, one and all, stink. . . . I really think that article was a great performance . . . but I do think that it omitted the stink and the sourness of Russia—so these notes have been written on the assumption that you are all familiar with *Fortune's* article and will use these notes simply as slight correctives of the focus."

Our passenger was a charmer, though. We got all our names straight, Johnny doing his usual pantomime (with only one hand on the wheel). The Russian's name was Vashoff (I'm guessing at the spelling). "Vash-off," whispered Tim, "I wish he would." Vashoff, however, was thrilled to know we were Americans, and openly admired our van. We concluded his "perfume" was a compost of one pint sour cream, one liter vodka, and no running water, all seasoned by a week of hard labor. I must say, we began to wonder with some misgiving how long our passenger would be with us. W. A. Swanberg's biography of Henry Luce records his (and our) frustration: "If one could talk with them, learn something from them, it would be different, but all we can do is smile and smell!" Lucid Luce—for once I agreed with him.

We came to the conclusion that the pervading odor can be directly attributed to diet, as we watched the Russians, not in sophisticated restaurants but in the smaller cities, put down gobs of onions, sour milk, sour cream, and, well, vodka.

We finally deposited Vashoff at his destination and continued with the truck parade. We had heard that vodka drinking was a serious problem in Russia, and by the time we reached Moscow we believed it. We saw ample evidence of drunken driving; at one point we barely missed involvement in a collision with a ten-ton truck. It came erratically toward us, just missed, then collided head-on with a small car behind us. At least on Saturdays, driving in Russia is hazardous to your health.

In the late afternoon we began to see more signs that read *Mockba—Moskva.* Moscow, to us. The Soviets sometimes (but not usually) find it necessary to print a city name in both alphabets. It was in Russia that we decided that proper names should never be translated. If the Russians call Moscow *Moskva,* why don't we? If the Austrians call their capital *Wien,* why do we say Vienna? After all, we don't call that great Austrian culinary specialty Vienna schnitzel.

We found it a real nuisance to have anglicized maps while traveling in a country where names are, naturally, printed native. The people on Crete have never heard of such an island; they think they live on Kríti.

We'd been 12 hours on the road when finally we intersected the "ring" that encircles Moscow. The Intourist office, we knew, was on Gorky Street, right near the Kremlin. Like a heat-seeking missile, the Beast flew down a spoke of the great wheel that is Moscow's street plan, headed for the hub, the power source. The streets of the city were smooth and wide open. Expecting to reach the center at any moment, we drove for what seemed like an hour. All six of us were crowded into the front of the car, our anticipation growing. We found Gorky Street without being aware of it, so didn't look for Intourist, observing only that this bustling boulevard was comparable to Park Avenue in New York or our own Michigan Avenue in Chicago. There were many taxicabs and many people. There were hotels and restaurants and shop displays. The city was vibrant. It was not until we were face to face with its red-hued walls that, leaving Gorky Street and breaking into a large square, we saw the Kremlin. Floodlit on this brittle October evening, it looked just like what it was: a fortress; and if not the heart of Russia (which we had already found in its people), then certainly the brain center, the source of the signals that make the muscles flex, sending ripples to Kiev, to Vladivostok, and around the earth.

We were to see the Kremlin many times during our brief visit to Moscow, from all angles possible, in the rain and in the sunshine; but never again did it convey the impact we felt that night as, after driving two days through dimlit hinterlands, we abruptly came upon the place where light was concentrated. We were intimidated. We parked and sat and looked.

But we still didn't know where we were going to eat or sleep, so we set our minds to the task of locating Intourist for instructions. That mission accomplished after what seemed an interminable search, we reversed our course and split for the perimeter to find our hotel.

As usual when we were in cities, Dan took over the porto position and the maps, allowing him to be next to Johnny's ear, the better to function as navigator. Dan was very good at guiding us around in strange places. Fortunately for us, during the long hours we had spent on the road during the past two days, he had taught himself to transliterate the Cyrillic alphabet. He declared that once you got onto it, it was very clear, and Russian was more logical than English because in its own alphabet it was completely phonetic. Not only that, but some words that looked upside down and backwards to us were actually *in English*. He had to prove *that* to us. He did.

We had learned by our second day in Russia that the word *pectopah* meant "restaurant." When its inventors introduced the Cyrillic alphabet in the 9th century as a convenient way to express the sounds of the Slavic languages, they did one dumb thing (from our point of view). They used some of "our" letters to mean "their" sounds. For example, a *P* in Cyrillic is really an R; a *C* is an S; and an *H* is an N. To confuse us further, *E, T, O,* and *A* are pronounced roughly as they are in English. So: If a *P* is an R and an *E* is an E, but a *C* is an S while a *T* is a T, and an *O* is an O, and a *P* still an R, with an *A* an A but an *H* an N . . . then *PECTOPAH* is RESTORAN!

But Dan couldn't find the hotel for us. It was fast approaching 10:00 P.M., and we were fast approaching the outer edges of Moscow, not to mention the younger kids' claim that they were fast approaching starvation. Again, our thoughtful Intourist representative had written the name of the hotel in "our" alphabet. Dan did the transliteration to Cyrillic according to his home-method. But we'd seen no such sign. When Dan noticed Johnny caressing his lower lip with the sharp edges of his upper teeth, he quickly suggested that we pull over in front of the next *pectopah*. "I will inquire of the Pectopites," Dan said.

As Dan later told us, it was a needlessly embarrassing experience. He said he must have been blind. Dan went in with the piece of paper on which he had written his version of the hotel name as well as Intourist's. The woman to whom he showed the paper smiled and nodded. Dan commenced to point, first one way down the street, then in the opposite direction, accompanying this pantomime with the hunched-shoulders-palms-up gesture which everywhere indicates a question—in this case, "Which way should we go?" The woman again nodded and smiled. She pointed to the desk across the room. On the desk was a sign that read "Mozhaiska Hotel." We were there. This was our hotel. We were "home."

We checked into three plain but clean dormlike rooms. The kids were overjoyed. Our Intourist plan generally called for three to a room, so this was real luxury for the same price. Plus the bathrooms were spotless. Despite our exhaustion, we washed up and went down to the dining room in great spirits. We had forgotten one little detail. It was Saturday night.

That was why the downtown streets had been so lively and that was also why the restaurant was jumping. Like every other tourist hotel we stayed in in Russia, this one had a band. Weekends were exceptional because, whereas on week *days* all those Russian men who seemed to be missing from the road gangs and fields could be found in the cafes sans female companionship, on Saturday nights they brought along the girls. And there were significant numbers of unescorted women.

We stood just inside the door of the restaurant, hoping that someone would come to seat us, although our experience had already led us not to count on it. The room was big, modern, and high-ceilinged; the band was on a raised platform to our right. On our left, beyond the swinging door leading to the kitchen, were small individual dining rooms, little more than booths made "private" by wine-colored draperies. Otherwise, I have no recollection of anything one might call "decor." The band was going full tilt, doing its best pseudo-decadent West; the room was full of happy, laughing people, none of whom appeared to be from our side of the world.

We were conspicuous for three reasons. First, our clothes, something we just couldn't help. They were never anything special; in fact, that evening we felt a little tacky. Yet I know we looked different. While we were dressed more casually than many in the room, our clothing fit better, was of better quality, and was generally more colorful—although I must say some in this Saturday-night crowd offered an exception. Then there were our children, who were always the only children in cafes. Last, though not necessarily in order of importance, was Debbie. On this evening she wore a robin's-egg blue miniskirt with a matching polka-dot blouse. With her blond hair hanging to her waist, her long, nyloned legs, and her bone-colored patent leather sandals . . . Well, it was just one of those nights. I had to look at her twice myself. A 15-year-old girl is funny that way; she can look or act 10 or 20. Tonight she looked 20. Before we sat down a gentleman came over to ask her to dance. She was terribly embarrassed and refused. Johnny told her that next time it might be handy to bring Gert-rude along.

After an uncomfortable wait of 20 minutes, we were finally led into one of the individual rooms. That, we thought, was good and bad. On the one hand, Deb was offered some protection; but on the other, it was going to be murder to get service, always a problem in Russian restaurants. We decided to relax. After all, the evening was young, as they say, and we had those clean rooms waiting for us upstairs and we could just sleep in next morning if this procedure were to take all night. As it turned out, it did indeed take all night.

Johnny's foot was aching—he thought he'd bruised it playing catch on the rocky roadside where we'd stopped for lunch that afternoon—so Tim asked me to dance. Tim loves to dance and does very well with any beat, even imitating the old ballroom styles with dips and swirls. But fundamentally, Tim's a child of rock. Five years ago, when Tim was about six, Johnny (who in turn had learned from Chicago Bear teammates J. C. Caroline and Roosevelt Taylor) taught him what Tim calls "my James Brown," a dance style that the great Brown himself would probably think was as "pseudo" as the music we were listening to. Tim's dance involves a lot of fancy footwork and movement from the waist down, the chest and shoulders limited mostly to a rhythmic sway with an occasional jerk for emphasis. He will sometimes do the whole thing with his thumbs hooked in his belt. What really fascinates me, though, is his soft, young face, with its look of total absorption in the music and commitment to the dance. If I get too close, his thatched head tickles the bottom of my chin.

Although Holly would make a much more sensible partner for Tim, he considers dancing with his little sister somewhat beneath his dignity. I more or less play bass fiddle to his Stradivarius, moving just enough to justify my presence on the dance floor; somehow he got born with a talent that skipped me.

The floor was crowded, but Tim doesn't need much room to do his thing; nevertheless, it wasn't long before I noticed that the other dancers were allowing us more space. Indeed, they were abandoning what Tim describes as the "Russian Hot-Foot Rock" and pulling back to watch the latest foreign import. When the music stopped and we walked back through the crunch of tables to our booth, several people smiled at Tim, a couple raising their hands over their heads in applause. "Are they clapping for us?" he asked incredulously.

It seemed they were, for the next thing we knew, a small, dark man, his mouth gleaming with gold teeth, was at our table congratulating Johnny, hugging Tim, bowing to me, and then going right back to Tim, his head shaking in wonder. He acted like Cecil B. De Mille discovering a future star.

By this time we had ordered a banquet, trying to use up all those meal coupons we'd had no time or place to spend on the road. Our hors d'oeuvres had arrived, but our friend showed no inclination to leave and we embarked on another of those non-language conversations, this one more fun than usual because Georgi Krekorian (names are easy to exchange) was a very colorful guy. He also considered himself a foreigner to Russia, even though he was from the Soviet republic of Armenia.

His mission, which it took a while to figure out, was to get Tim and me to dance an exhibition. He pointed to his friends (a table of six red-faced, good-natured, but wild-looking men), indicating they thought Tim was a little superman; from Georgi's gestures I felt like he was saying, "This kid's some little stud."

The hardest thing to get across was our nationality. Georgi thought we were Finns (always the Russians' first guess). Johnny kept saying, "U.S.," "U.S.A.," "United States." The magic word, however, was "America." Georgi finally comprehended. His eyes rolled back and he pointed around the room, now unsmiling. *"Americanski?"* he said. We nodded apprehensively. "Ahhhh . . . soooo," he breathed. Georgi seemed to think for a minute, then evidently forgave us our origins, for he was soon bouncing around as before, his attention centered on Tim.

When Tim finally got the message that he was being asked to go on stage, he began to shake his head stubbornly. *"Nyet, nyet, nyet,"* he said. But Georgi wouldn't take *nyet* for an answer. He called the hostess and spoke rapidly as he laid a fistful of rubles on her. Then he called a waitress and issued more orders. Like magic our food began to arrive. Georgi picked this time to insist that Tim and I get up.

Just as we did, the band played a drumroll, and we deduced, as Georgi shoved us through the crowd, that the bandleader was announcing our exhibition. Tim was still saying *nyet,* and for a moment I thought he would lose his composure. "We have no choice, Tim," I told him. The spotlight was on. The noisy room grew quiet.

The band's blast almost instantly converted Tim to "James Brown," and our troubles were over. I must say he rose to the occasion while I almost fell with it. After five minutes, I turned myself toward the band leader and gave him the international knock-it-off-sign—a slicing motion, the hand across the throat. Fortunately, that gesture is understood in the Soviet Union, and I was saved from humiliation by exhaustion. As we returned to the family, who had emerged with Georgi from our private booth to stand and watch, many people rose and shouted bravos while others clapped and even threw kisses.

On our table, the cold food had been joined by two chilled bottles of Georgian champagne and a stack of chocolate bars. I wondered what James Brown would make of it all. At 12:30 A.M., after an altogether confusing and enjoyable evening, we stumbled up to our rooms. I marveled at Holly. She was still conscious.

Moscow is a great city. *It is.* It has most everything a tourist would want in a city. The public transportation is excellent, and it's easy to get around. There are a million things to see, things different enough from what we are accustomed to in the West to make them extra interesting. And it's not terribly expensive.

Nevertheless, we had our moments of desperation. One of them was shared by Tim and Johnny, although each claimed to be the greater sufferer. At the Hotel Leningrad, Johnny had embarrassed Tim by performing one of his by-now expert pantomimes for a lady clerk, this time to explain his urgent need for a laxative. It hadn't worked (the pantomime, that is). Tim, totally humiliated, had run the moment the shocked look crossed the lady's face. So when Johnny threatened to go shopping again, Tim quickly suggested The Dad write for a good old U.S. remedy instead. Since I had just finished a letter to my parents, The Flanker decided he would add a paragraph describing his distress, closing with, "To be serene is to love thy system, and I am not serene. . . . *Please send pills."* (Johnny's "relief" finally did arrive, though not until we were in Yugoslavia.)

Johnny was beginning to realize that he would need to seek out a doctor about his worsening foot ailment which, it developed, was more than a bruise. Like many of his colleagues from the world of sport, he has been plagued for years with athlete's foot. Mostly it's dormant, but every once in a while it breaks out. Now it had become infected and was not responding to standard treatment. Johnny was a little worried, but accustomed as he was to "playing with pain," he somehow hung in there and we saw a lot of Moscow, including a day-long tour of the city, a night at the opera, and a frustrating and unproductive search through the shops for something to send home.

One of the "benefits" of the Soviet system is that medical attention is free—and it's worth every kopeck of it. We finally went to the office of the "doctor for foreigners" whom Maie, a valued newfound friend employed at the Mozhaiska Hotel, had told us about. After a five-hour wait—stretched over two separate days—Johnny saw the doctor. *She* was 60 years old, and I know, I just know, Johnny let his chauvinism show. Not only that, but he said he told the doctor, "At home, *my* doctor gives me an ointment that clears it all right up," and snapped his fingers to show the superiority of American medicine. Now, I ask you, was that politic? Anyhow, the net result was that "the old lady" said "Tut, tut, tut" (in Russian); dabbed on some disinfectant and a little salve; wrapped his foot in gauze "clear above my ankle"; and prescribed a medicine that cost a very reasonable one ruble and, I swear, smelled just like cocoa butter. "You do, you really do; in Russia you do get what you pay for . . . you know you do," moaned my poor old sportscaster.

According to Johnny's interpretation, his Moscow dermatologist's instructions were to change the bandage twice a day, each time cleaning the wound with alcohol and daubing on a solution derived from dissolving a pill the doctor had given him. Then we were to cover the infected area with the prescribed goop and rewrap the foot. No matter how slowly and gently I did all this, it was to the tune of shrill instructions, Johnny's understandable irritation a result of worry as much as pain. The gauze became embedded, and despite soaking, removal was excruciating.

At first, the kids would sit by and try to make him laugh, sometimes succeeding. As the condition grew worse, though, he would send them out because he knew he was going to cuss. Sometimes Dan stayed back to hold Johnny's leg.

We found no way to make the pills dissolve, in hot or cold water. Johnny thought now that he might have misunderstood, maybe the pills were to be taken by mouth? Dan suggested he'd be dumb to put a pill in his stomach that wouldn't dissolve in water. So we tossed the pills.

I asked Johnny how this "hurt" compared to knee surgery, broken clavicle, pulled groin muscles, and hip pointers of football days. He was evasive—said at least he didn't ever remember being reinjured by a bandage.

No question about it, we had problems. And this grim foot thing didn't make the difficult and tedious drive from Moscow to Kiev any easier. But something about the problems we all shared turned the kids into troupers. They knew by this time that nothing was to be done about Soviet conditions. And we had our van.

I think I would have loved Kiev, had I seen it. Our view of Kiev was from the inside of a Russian medical clinic. This time, following another hectic wait and infinite translation problems (finally solved when we ran into 6-foot 5-inch identical twin brothers named Anthony and George, Russians who spoke English), Johnny drew a male doctor, a surgeon. The doctor's treatment was quite direct. He took a small scalpel and sliced through the infected area (about half the bottom of Johnny's foot) and dragged alcohol-soaked gauze through the wound over and over again. Johnny yelled so loud I was looking over my shoulder for the K.G.B. He told me later that, as relatively minor as he knew the problem to be, it was the sharpest pain he had ever experienced.

Since The Flanker spent practically the whole day with those adorable 21-year-old twins, the three of them got to know quite a bit about each other. Apparently one of the twins had told the doctor that Johnny was a former professional athlete. So when Johnny screamed in pain, the doctor and nurse started jabbering in Russian. Johnny's face was flushed, and he was mad. "What's going on?" he shouted in confusion. "What's this isik, ibit visthik stuff?" he said, mouthing a string of nonsense syllables that seemed to him a fair imitation of Russian. There was a moment of quiet, then George translated, "The doctor says, 'Big American football player, huh?' "

The good doctor then offered a continuing prescription translated by twin George as "spirits on the foot and spirits in the mouth." There was nothing to do but continue that spirited treatment—which I performed twice a day—until a Polish doctor finally rescued us both.

We decided to forego one day's worth of prepaid food and lodging in Russia. I really would have liked to stay over another day in Lvov, a rich, fascinating city in pre-"Great Patriotic War" Poland, but the kids would have none of it, and Johnny wanted to get to Warsaw as soon as possible. He had no idea what the Polish medical setup was like ("At least I've never heard a joke about it," he said), but he figured it had to be an improvement over the Russian system. Johnny thought his foot was getting worse rather than better. Indeed, the infected area seemed as big and angry as ever.

During the hour or so it took us to reach the border that morning, I was consumed with a feeling of frustration. I felt like turning back, doing it all again but finding a way to do it better. I couldn't sort out our experiences. I didn't think I'd learned much. I wondered if the children had gotten anything out of the past two weeks aside from discomfort. Johnny was saying *already* that what he remembered most about Russia was his foot. I knew Tim had dropped at least five pounds, a lot for a little boy, and from the way my clothes were hanging I thought I'd lost about eight, which was OK. But we lost the weight the hard way—nausea and diarrhea.

As we look back now, a year later, we wouldn't have missed it, the occasional travail notwithstanding. We came away with powerful impressions about the tremendous strength of the Soviet Union and the way the system works. Much as we resented the State-decreed restrictions, the Russian people were just great. They loved the children. They were usually pleased and excited to learn we were Americans. They ohhed and ahhed and lined up to stare at the Beast and laugh at The Dad's pantomime describing its marvelous features. And we saw much evidence of striving for material improvement, both by the government and by individuals, legions of whom were small-scale capitalists.

But I cannot overemphasize how the details of living and driving in the Soviet Union override all else in our memories ... the three skuz hotels we had to use on the road, the tired peasant faces, the huge military presence, the women without men walking arm in arm, the truck traffic, the female road gangs, the old man begging us for chewing gum, the young man who wanted to buy all of our clothes, the border searches, the endless paperwork. There were absolutely no restaurants or comfort facilities on those long, long stretches of Russian road. But there was always vodka and the feared drunken driver. If they've got a grain problem, they ought to start milling the stuff and stop distilling it. Driving at night was near impossible since headlights weren't allowed, but we had to do it numerous times because the schedule decreed by Intourist made incredible demands on its clients.

But on the day we were to check out of Russia, Johnny was just plain worried as he rolled the Beast up to straddle a deep concrete pit, following the border guard's request. Just as at the northern border, a modern building housed the customs station. But across from us was Poland, not Finland, so there was no need for a buffer zone with its bristling communications tower and soldiers; and there was only one gate.

Johnny asked the kids to sit in the car while we went in to see what the checkout routine would be. The atmosphere in the station may have been relaxed, but Johnny wasn't. While the guards outside climbed around and underneath the van with flashlights and probers, we were instructed to bring in all of our bags. We did, but they were barely searched. Meanwhile, Tim and Holly had left the car and were running in, out, and around the station, venting steam that I hadn't realized Tim, at least, had left in him. At one point Johnny came close to knocking their heads together, so great was his tension.

For a long time, nothing at all happened. We were told to wait. The bags had been looked at, the car checked on the outside, and the guards had taken a cursory look inside. Our documents had been in the back room for an hour when Johnny decided he would need his ace in the hole. From his pocket he took a folded piece of paper on which the lovely Maie of the Mozhaiska had written for us just before we left Moscow. We had no way of knowing whether she had translated precisely as Johnny had dictated, but he'd outlined a letter addressed to the border guards, explaining our entire family mission. In a word, it protested our innocence: We had our whole year's household in that van. A woman guard who had been very cordial looked at the letter; about halfway through, she began to laugh. She signaled the others to come over and they, too, joined in the merriment. Abruptly she went into the back room and retrieved our documents, indicating that we could go.

"Come on, come on, come on," Johnny was urging quietly, rounding up the kids. We climbed into the Beast and looked back through the plate glass windows. The lady guard was still smiling. She waved. So did we. The female gardening crew, busy giving the border station's rose garden a fall trimming, unbent to wave and smile. The single gate lifted. And we rolled west into the Peoples Republic of Poland.

We saw our first Polish billboard just beyond the Russian border. We had been through two weeks and 2,600 miles of posters showing peasant-faces-with-chins-uptilted-in-grim-determination; the Polish sign read simply, "Pepsi Cola." The kids went bananas.

"No Probe-lem"

Warsaw was absolutely booked with a big Communist Workers Convention when we arrived, and the campgrounds were closed. But John the Con and his ally finally saved the day. I had tried three hotels before Johnny dragged himself out of the Beast and limped into the fourth on Holly's arm. Together they got us two rooms; they said it was easy.

Has anyone ever told you how beautiful Poland is? I WILL NEVER LISTEN TO ANOTHER POLISH JOKE. A moonlighting Polish doctor finally got Johnny's foot on the path to recovery, and we continued on our way through Eastern Europe.

I don't know *what* in our meager travel experience gave us the feeling that when we got to Yugoslavia we'd be home, but the minute we left Budapest we were like horses with a sniff of the barn. I suppose it was because our visit to Russia, Poland, Czechoslovakia, and Hungary had required somewhat rigid schedules, and travel deadlines are tiring. We discovered that what exhausts people when they travel is not the seeing and doing itself, but trying to see and do too much in too short a time. We ran into a lot of exhausted Americans. Right now, *we* were exhausted Americans.

Our goal was Dubrovnik, the "Pearl of the Adriatic," the ancient walled city which we pictured as basking in sunlight by a warm sea. Our route from Belgrade through the mountains to the Moslem-dominated city of Sarajevo and down to the Adriatic coast was so fascinating that we just dawdled along, watching the steady trains of pack mules, seeing turbaned loggers work their long poles in the eddies of the Drina River, eating spit-roasted lamb by the roadside, and visiting with an 80-year-old coppersmith as he warmed his cracked hands over a charcoal brazier in his tiny shop on a narrow alley of Sarajevo's Turkish bazaar.

From Sarajevo we traveled west across the mountain spine of Yugoslavia, then followed the green Neretva River through barren, dramatic gorges and down into a great plain that produces, among other things, the fine wines of Mostar. We'd read that the roads of Yugoslavia were difficult, but we never found them so. Of course things get very relative on a trip like ours. We'd just completed a long ride through the Soviet Union, an experience guaranteed to make the Burma Road seem like the Pennsylvania Turnpike.

The Yugoslavs have a favorite saying that is kind of nice and goes something like this: "Yugoslavia has six republics, five peoples, four languages, three religions, two alphabets—and one desire for peace." In the eventual course of two visits, we spent almost three months in Yugoslavia and saw much of this fascinating mélange.

But it was something I saw on that narrow mountain road as we pushed west toward the Adriatic that still says Yugoslavia to me. Three generations of women were walking toward us beside the asphalt. The youngest, a teenager, had on blue jeans and a bright peasant blouse; her mother was dressed in a tweed skirt and "sensible" shoes; and grandma wore great Moslem pantaloons, which swirled in the mountain breezes. The old lady's stringy gray hair escaped her babushka, and I could see she had no teeth because she was laughing past her daughter at something her tanned, young granddaughter was saying. The three women remain an enchanting freeze frame in my mind.

Wandering down the Adriatic coast from where the Neretva meets the sea to Dubrovnik was one of those head-swiveling experiences. "Look at this!" "See that!" "Mom!" "Dad!" "What is it?" A potential problem in Yugoslavia is a sore neck.

A few miles north of Dubrovnik we found the Orasac International campground. Set in an old olive orchard, it was terraced down to 50-foot cliffs that plunged into the Adriatic. There were beautiful private campsites, a small store, and a lovely restaurant built in a reconstructed old castle. There was one problem: The campground was closed. We found out that camping in Yugoslavia is only permitted in official campgrounds and that these are only open from May to September. It was now the first week of November.

This restriction was news to us. We had enjoyed some beautiful nights of camping, all the way from Belgrade. And as a matter of fact, the image of that delicious "forbidden" campground at Orasac never did leave our minds, and we returned there the following April and spent three perfect days—until the police found us and (politely) kicked us out.

Our problem now was to find good, cheap lodging. That, it happened, was not difficult because about any Yugoslav on the Dalmatian coast who can get the money together has built an extra room or two onto his house and rents it whenever possible. This is one of the fascinating facets of President Tito's brand of Communism. Beginning in the home, Yugoslavia is rife with aggressive, acquisitive capitalists.

We finally laid our heads down for a long-sought rest, not in Dubrovnik, but in its neighbor to the south, a sparkling curl of a fishing village called Cavtat. In season, Cavtat would have many more tourists than fish, but in November it was quiet. There we were able to rent the top half of a villa, a fully-furnished, three-bedroom, two-bath home with a kitchen and living room, a patio, three seaward terraces, and a private beach—well, a concrete swimming and fishing dock built into the rocky cliff. The charge was $3 per day per person; in season, our new home rented for $60 per. It was almost Christmas before we left Cavtat.

Our landlord, Josip Robic, his wife, Maria, and daughter, Tamara, lived on the first floor of the house, an equally beautiful apartment. Josip was a minor hotel functionary, and every day after work he would visit us, exchanging experiences, spinning tales. We spent the entire six weeks trying to figure out how Josip and many, many Yugoslavs like him managed to live like millionaires on small wages in a communist country. On the face of it, and by any standard, Josip had it made.

The only thing of note we did in Cavtat was live there.

Ordinarily we went to the market every day, partly because it was fun and partly because we were addicted to fragrant, fresh bread. Fresh bread is one of the many luxuries one finds commonly only in "less advanced" countries.

I always rose just before the sun rose, my favorite time of the day, a time to see the sea glisten pink. Dotting the water off Yugoslavia's coast are more than a thousand islands and islets that serve as a natural breakwater; and when there is no wind, the already calm Adriatic is like a lake. Later on during our stay, when it grew colder and my first dawn duty was to light a wood fire in the fireplace (we had no heat), there was a whole new sea to watch—a sea touched by the Bora.

I particularly remember one November day when we had a lashing storm that seemed to be punishing the coast head-on. We'd lost our electricity by 7 o'clock in the evening and so went to bed by candlelight, listening to the crash and roar of the surf directly below our bedroom terrace. It was one of the few times when Josip's blankets were not warm enough, and Johnny and I were tucked into our sleeping bags, separate islands on a king-sized bed. Sometime during the night I was startled awake—by a sudden, absolute stillness.

In the morning I saw for the first time the effects of the wind they call the Bora. It blows from the east and does strange things to Yugoslavia, adding to the country's infinite variety. The Bora skips over nearly all the coastal resorts, including Cavtat; when it hits the mountains, its altered trajectory takes the wind's first bite further out to sea. While most of Yugoslavia's islands are lush with vegetation, those that know the Bora are barren rocks.

On this morning in late November, the crashing sounds of the previous day had been replaced by a sort of whistling. The wind seemed to be blowing harder than ever, but was missing our tucked-in village. The water, which on a clear day ranged from turquoise to deep blue in color, was now gray. The sea was without swells or waves, its surface flat, yet swirling, as if a giant helicopter were hovering overhead, forcing the wind straight down. Far out, I could see a few places where the Bora touched directly, creating masses of white water. In other spots, funnels rose as tiny whirlwinds and scampered toward the islands. On mornings such as this, before my family and the sun got up to add their warmth, I would sit and shiver, but never tire of watching the strangeness of the Bora.

Unless we had a special program planned, the number-one activity after a light breakfast was school. Johnny would assign Tim and Holly to separate rooms and begin their lessons, while Dan and Deb and I, after a few household chores, would settle down to reading and writing. Two things never ceased to astound me. The first was Johnny's unflagging enthusiasm for schoolteaching, and the second was Dan's and Deb's powerful yen to record events in their diaries. And one of our biggest problems on the trip, one I enjoyed having, was keeping all four of the kids supplied with reading material. A year without television is a wondrous thing.

Around 11 o'clock we would hop into the Beast and go to the open market in Gruz, one of the many neighborhoods surrounding Dubrovnik's commercial wharfs, where the locals do their shopping. Josip always told us that the only time to go to market was at 5:00 A.M., when the farmers were setting up their stalls. We never made it; but when Josip was on the early shift, he would stop and shop at dawn, on his way to work, returning home for lunch with bundles of fresh fruit and vegetables and often flowers for Maria. By hard bargaining we could usually get a fair price reduction in the market; but Josip, loaded with natural charm and finesse, was a champ. He also bought his milk, eggs, meat, and wine directly from farmers around Dubrovnik. This all took time, of course; but with Maria's talent in the kitchen, the Robics were able to set a tasty fresh table that was better than any amount of money can buy in most places.

There were two supermarkets in Dubrovnik—at least they were called supermarkets. While a Russian housewife entering a Yugoslav grocery might think she had died and gone to heaven, such a store

would seem bare to, say, an urban Swede. Still, there were some
frozen vegetables, a portion of the meat was refrigerated, and there
was a variety of canned fruits and vegetables. Imports were irregularly
available—and expensive. Canned mushrooms from France, for example, cost over $2 and so did furniture polish from England. I
never did find anything that would adequately clean the bathroom.
Nevertheless, you could shop for most of your food needs in one place
and pay one cashier, and that in itself was a considerable advancement
in convenience over many other European countries.

Sometimes the entire city would run out of the same product all
at once. One cynical American we ran into, a rich expatriate who
was "wintering" on his yacht in Dubrovnik, told us the reason retail-
ing was "so screwed up" was that the markets were state-owned and
the buying was done collectively, so a product sometimes remained
unordered until the city ran out collectively. Once, he said, Dubrovnik
ran out of toilet paper. "That was no loss," Tim told him, since
regular Yugoslav toilet paper could be replaced by any old newspaper.

After lunch, if the weather was good, we'd swim or fish or both.
A natural fisherwoman, Holly spent literally hours sitting on the dock
hooking tiny fish which she fed to a cat she had befriended. Sometimes Johnny or Dan would don the snorkling gear and dive near her
bait to watch the fish nibble, then give Holly an arm signal indicating
when she should jerk the line and set her hook. And so it was that
Holly fattened the cat.

One afternoon I went to a beauty shop—for the first time since
leaving the States. There were no appointments, I was told, "just go
and sit." It happened that I went and sat on the day before a holiday.
There were seven girls working in a room that *might* have been
adequate for three operators, and at one time I counted 15 customers
in the place. All of the women were local and mostly they were
laughing and gossiping. Fortunately for me, one of the operators
spoke a little English, and I was able to tell her what I wanted done
to my hair. There was already one woman being worked on in the
middle of the room, and when another chair was found, I, too, took
center stage. It was like a bumper-car game, with women rushing
into each other as the operators dashed from sink to mirror to dryer.
I was lost in a circle of shrill Serbo-Croatian, the principal language
of Yugoslavia. One very fat lady was having her eyebrows shaved

(beauty shops do a big business in hair removal, as Yugoslav women seem to have a problem with mustaches, etc.) and, through no fault but her own, came close to being blinded a couple of times by the gal who was working on her. She must have been the Joan Rivers of the crowd: By the gestures she was making, I'd swear that she was telling dirty jokes, and the whole room was breaking up. After three hours my hair had been washed, cut, frosted, set, combed, and dried. The woman had done a good job—the price was $6. Back home, on Michigan Avenue, they get $70 for the same treatment (and no jokes).

Dinner in our Cavtat home might be *raznjici,* a sort of shish kabob, cooked on our small charcoal grill, with rice and raw onions and a huge platter of fresh vegetables. Always we would have wine, and sometimes a sweet for dessert. Debbie invented a great cookie which she more or less bribed us with since she refused to reveal the recipe and would only make them when the whim struck her.

The hours after dinner were the most fun—that's when Josip and sometimes Tamara visited. Maria would never come because, although she spoke fluent German, her English, at least in her view, was a bit awkward. Actually, nothing much got by Maria in any language. Josip was not shy at all. A tile stairway connected our apartments, and Josip might come shuffling up the stairs in his peculiarly graceful style and walk right into the living room without so much as a tap on the door. This habit, exercised at all times of the day and night, at first disturbed us; later we looked forward to such "intrusions."

Depending on whether it was before or after his dinner, Josip would take warm scotch (before) or wine (after). The true hospitality drink in Croatia is *slivovica,* a plum brandy. But it's a real whacker, and after a taste or two we reverted to whiskey and wine.

One evening Josip came up all excited. There was to be a great American film on TV that night called "Midday Shoot." "Midday Shoot?" We'd never heard of it. He said it was famous, a cowboy movie. We knew we'd seen every famous cowboy movie ever made. "Midday Shoot?" Then Josip said the film "won America's big movie prize," and the star was Gary Cooper. "High Noon"! The kids just broke up laughing and Josip shrugged. It was one of his theories that one should never speak a foreign tongue perfectly. Josip said that he almost resented the unusual circumstance of hearing a foreigner speak Serbo-Croatian perfectly. He asked one evening, "Do you not think it is more . . . more charming if I speak in English some things slightly wrong?" Besides, he added, in the language of Yugoslavia there is no such expression as "High Noon."

Josip's favorite American television import was "Columbo." (It plays weekly, and as in the case of "Midday Shoot," is subtitled in Serbo-Croatian.) Now, if you will picture Police Lieutenant Columbo —slow but quick, sweet but steely—then straighten the lieutenant's eyes and put a twinkle in them, and substitute an off-buttoned sweater for the slouchy raincoat, you will have a picture of Josip Robic. Like Columbo, Josip was effective because his manner belied his ability, range of knowledge, and experience. Josip claimed to be apolitical, but had strong political opinions. He said he was a simple man of simple tastes, but he'd traveled to every important power center in the world. He'd built himself a six-bedroom, four-bath villa that would have made a Rockefeller proud, and rarely strayed into the old walled city of Dubrovnik, where he had grown up in a family of 11 children. His wife was not only beautiful but also a talented artist. His daughter wore genuine Levi's, and his little dog wore a Hartz 90-Day flea collar—both "impossible" to buy in Yugoslavia. Josip was a closet capitalist.

And he had a favorite saying: "No problem" (pronounced "no probe-lem"). That's what he said the first time all the taps ran dry and our wonderful villa was without water. "There is a little bubble in the line," Josip explained. "It will pass, and we will have water once more." It passed—after 36 hours. "No problem," he said again one night, walking in with an armload of candles as we sat reading by firelight because the electricity had blinked off. In Yugoslavia, technology is not quite up to speed. But Josip was right—for us it was no problem.

When the letter came from Lou and Jean Malnati, close friends from Chicago, telling us they would meet us in Rome on December 5, we faced a tough choice. By that time we had decided we would spend Christmas in the Yugoslav ski resort of Kranjska Gora in the Alps, close to the Austrian border. Rome was not exactly on the route to Kranjska Gora. Should we alter our plans entirely and spend Christmas in the Italian Alps?

The kids didn't want to go to Rome at all. Dan and Debbie

begged us to fly away to Rome and let them remain at the villa with Tim and Holly. They said they could handle everything and absolutely promised they would not bother Josip and Maria. Josip put in his two cents: "No problem," he said.

And so it was with sizable misgivings mixed with a powerful desire to keep our date with the Malnatis that we took off for what turned out to be a genuine Roman Holiday.

Except we didn't exactly take off. On December 3 we caught Josip covering his rose bushes and bringing his rubber plants inside. "Are you thinking it might freeze?" we asked. "It never does, but it might," he said, talking like a Southern Californian. On December 4 it snowed. On December 5 when we went out to catch our airplane, it flew right over our heads, not pausing in Dubrovnik because there was snow on the runway. We jumped in a taxi and drove madly back into the city, found we could catch a ferry to Bari, Italy, at midnight, and cabbed back to Cavtat. The kids' faces fell when they saw us. "Aren't you going?" they pleaded. We assured Dan that at 10:00 P.M. he and Tim could drive us to the wharf. The Malnatis were already aloft, en route from Chicago, and there was no turning back.

A few hours later Johnny and I found ourselves on another pitching, rolling ferryboat, but we were so tired that we slept five good hours before disembarking at 7:00 A.M. in a drizzly mist on the scruffy docks of Bari. We walked a half-mile in the rain, carrying our suitcases to customs. It was the first time we'd set foot in Italy, and we had no idea how we would reach Rome and the Malnatis from where we were. We called their hotel, the Cavalieri Hilton and left a message for our friends: "We're on our way." That's all we knew. If we chose to take a train, we would arrive in Rome in 11 hours. Unthinkable. Another cab ride to the airport and we caught the next commuter flight to Rome.

Our carefully constructed budget was going straight to hell.

Little Luciano Giuseppe Ernesto Malnati was born in Varese near Milan in northern Italy in 1929. At age nine he was slated to follow his father to America, but his mother became ill, and the departure was delayed. By the time she died, Benito Mussolini had joined Hitler and World War II was beginning to affect the lives of everyone in Europe. And so Luciano lived with his grandmother in Varese and spent his early teens guiding, scouting, and otherwise engaging in activities of the Partisans who opposed the Facist forces in the Italian Alps near Varese and Lake Como. After the war, with little but the clothes on his back and a promise that the father he hardly remembered would meet him in New York, young Lou's grandmother shipped him off to America.

Now it was 28 years later, and standing in the middle of the poshest lobby we'd seen since setting our sneakered feet on the continent of Europe was a rotund, red-haired man, no longer "Little" Luciano. Naturally, our Lou held a touch of the sauce in one hand. The other hand was plunged into the pocket of his plaid slacks—probably fingering a couple of thousand dollars secured in a gold money clip. A white turtleneck shirt seemed to support—without the help of a neck—the full, freckled face, and brown button eyes sparkled behind horn-rimmed glasses.

Naturally, he was talking. Loudly, naturally. The upper right side of his body, his arm and shoulder, seemed unnaturally shrunken. Beside him was his wife, Jean, the corner of her mouth tucked up in her listening-to-Lou expression, one of amusement mixed with irritation.

The Malnatis were the first friends or loved ones we'd seen—besides the six of us—in four months. Luciano Giuseppe Ernesto Malnati, our All-American friend, whose philosophy is "The Best Things in Life Are Expensive—and you damn well better let me pay for them."

Our Big Spender from the West had a problem that he (and we, and a thousand others in Chicago) prayed had been solved by radical surgery just two months earlier. We'd found out Lou had cancer while we were in Belgrade. We had called his restaurant (Luciano is known as "The Pizza King" in Chicago) to congratulate him during the third annual Brian Piccolo Scholarship party. Lou throws this party every year to raise money for a scholarship fund in the name of the late Chicago Bear running back, who died of cancer in 1970.

The Piccolo party is not like other benefits: The Pizza King absorbs all the overhead so that the entire $25 admission price goes to the Piccolo Scholarship. Lou's theme: "Let a boy continue." Brian would have loved that—and he would have loved the party, traditionally a wild, noisy, happy affair. It was certainly wild that night when, half-way around the world in Belgrade, we heard Lou say over the crackling telephone, "Hey, Flanker, you know what? I got cancer too."

Lou is a great hugger and kisser and backslapper, and because of this, people who come into his restaurants are always hugging and kissing and backslapping him back. With this daily punishment, although it had been two months since his operation, the scabbardlike incision that ran from the middle of Lou's back down and under his armpit had not yet completely healed. He stripped off his shirt and showed us the scar that evening in Rome. "Ain't that a bitch?" he said. The words twisted my heart; it was precisely the expression Piccolo had used when he showed his first surgical scar to his friend Gale Sayers.

But the scar-showing was the end of it for Luciano. He had only a week in Rome and he wasn't about to spend it moping around about a pimple of a melanoma. So what do you think The Pizza King does in the Pasta Capital? Look at ruins? Are you kidding? He eats.

Since Johnny and I would be returning to Rome in the spring with the children, it was OK by us to follow the Malnati itinerary. However, considering our own proclivities, Johnny and I got one important break: The energy crisis had forced an 11:00 P.M. curfew, and Roman restaurants at that time were observing it closely. Ordinarily, 11 o'clock is dinnertime for Lou . . . and bedtime is between 3:00 A.M. and 5:00 A.M. We never have been able to keep his pace.

When the Malnatis are in Italy, they are accustomed to enjoying the services and Mercedes limousine of one Renato Polidori. Renato is an international chauffeur, licensed to drive all the roads of Europe. But Renato, along with a considerable portion of the Italian labor force, was on strike. This made Luciano almost as unhappy as it made Renato, who knew he was missing a good time—as well as a till-filling week. Nevertheless, it became a ritual that between lunch (1:00 P.M. to 4:00 P.M.) and dinner (usually 7:00 P.M. to 11:00 P.M.), Renato would bounce up to the hotel on Monte Mario in his wife's Fiat to join us in the Cavalieri Hilton bar for a touch of the grape and a report on the "progress" of the strike. Had it not been for the fact that "Signor Malnati" was a "special customer," Renato wouldn't have minded the strike, because Italy's truckers had also walked out, and what gasoline there was, was not reaching the filling stations.

Roman cabbies, when we could find one, were in a foul mood; they had to wait in long lines for a fuel allotment that would only keep them on the street for a couple of hours. Also, the price of gasoline was up to $1.52 per gallon.

Renato told us a story about an Arab oil official for whom he'd driven the previous month. The Arab said the Italians of all people had little room to complain, because even at today's prices they paid less per liter for oil than they did for their precious *acqua minerale* (mineral water), without which, it seems, an Italian cannot enjoy a meal.

It was a bit difficult for us to try not to be preoccupied with Lou's illness or with our kids, left behind in an unheated house in Cavtat; but going first class was such a change that our Roman Holiday had Cinderella aspects. After one colossal, Malnati-style (shouting, screaming) argument, we settled our financial arrangement: Johnny would pick up the tabs one day, Lou the next. Of course, that didn't include tips—Lou's tips. Johnny is a 15 percent tipper; Lou would tip a guy for the privilege of stepping on his shadow.

Take Nino, for example. Nino was the 6-foot 5-inch, 150-pound doorman at the Hilton. With his size 15 shoes, he looked like my vision of Ichabod Crane. Lou laid a couple of thousand lira on Nino every time we walked in or out of the hotel. And Jean seemed surprised that Nino remembered them from the last time they had been in Rome, just the year before!

I'm not sure we had *ever* seen food cooked and displayed as it was in Rome; certainly, we had seen nothing approaching it since our last day in Scandinavia on September 30. That first afternoon at Maestrostefano on Piazza Navona, we ate and laughed over an exquisite meal until the yawning waiters and empty room embarrassed us into leaving. The bill for lunch—with wine, of course—was about $50. It was Johnny's day to pay.

The following afternoon we actually saw a "sight," the Fountain of Trevi. To be perfectly truthful, we tripped over the Trevi looking for an expensive restaurant. However, just down from the fountain on Via Dei Crociferi, we happened upon an intriguing-looking place called Ristorante La Toscana. Three of us wanted to lunch there, but The Pizza King refused. Unfortunately, the menu was posted on the door, and the prices, he said, were too cheap. This time, Johnny yelled louder than Lou, and we went in. To salve his conscience, Lou slipped the waiter 10,000 lira as we sat down.

Naturally the waiter, who looked about 70, started running; but speed never interested Lou at mealtime. He placed our order in Italian and cautioned the now sweating old man, *"Piano, piano"* (we want to eat slowly). We did. Had Lou not tipped so generously, I'm sure we would have been charged rent.

One morning while Jean and I shopped for boots to take back to little Tammy Robic in Yugoslavia, Lou slipped up the Via Veneto to sip a brandy at Doneys, the world-famous "see-and-be-seen" sidewalk cafe. He returned shortly, all het up and complaining that "every *finocchio* in Rome was eyeballing me." We figured out what *finocchio* meant. Literally, according to Lou, it translated "crooked celery." "What is it about me?" he asked. Could it have been his red alpaca cardigan over white turtleneck over tartan slacks that attracted attention?

Guidebooks give a lot of attention to "native costume." In Cilipi, for example, a village near Dubrovnik, the big attraction is the fact that the men almost always wear black pantaloons and flat hats and the women wear long, aproned dresses and immaculate white headpieces. They especially wear these costumes on Sunday, when the tourists come to visit.

Americans, however, are the only people we could find besides Indians from India who wear their native costumes abroad. I'm not referring to the classic business suit, a worldwide fashion, but to the costume that must have had its inception in Miami Beach or Palm Springs. It is worn only by the male of the American species, and its fundamental feature is plaid, checkered, or otherwise brightly colored pants, generally topped by an equally flamboyant sweater or combination of sweaters. There's nothing wrong with this, but when the itinerary says "casual dress," the affluent American on tour inevitably breaks out the plaid pants. This costume makes the American male the most totally identifiable tourist the world over.

Somehow Renato had gotten permission (we didn't ask how; the strike was still on) to drive us the day we traveled out the Appian Way into the hills behind Castel Gandolfo, the summer residence of Popes, to a restaurant called La Foresta. Chauffeur-friend Renato had bright blue eyes, dark "dry look" hair, and a direct, if slightly detached, gaze. Like Josip's, his English was just incorrect enough to be charming. Josip, too, had spent several years as a chauffeur for tourists. In Europe, chauffeuring is one of those activities—like taking speech in school—that no matter what you do the rest of your life, the experience is bound to help. I spent most of the 25-mile ride out to La Foresta spinning mental sit-coms with a dashing international chauffeur as hero.

La Foresta was absolutely beautiful—and deserted. There were still lamb, beef, and pork on the spit, and plenty of people to serve it . . . but no customers. Of course, it was a Thursday. Lou talked "restaurant talk" (in Italian) with the owner, who said that the bulk of his business came on weekends and the Sunday ban on driving was killing him. As for the other days of the week, the price and short supply of fuel weren't helping, either.

At 4 o'clock in the afternoon, Lou looked at his watch and declared: "It's time to call Wally." Wally is Wally Phillips. You might say he's a disk jockey, but he's more like an institution in Chicago—at least when he's on the air, from 6 o'clock to 10 o'clock every morning. Next thing we knew, Lou was shouting into the phone to Phillips, telling a WGN-Radio audience that he, Lou Malnati, had found Johnny Morris in Rome and that the old Bears flanker had grown a beard, carried a purse, and had turned into a "goddam finocchio." Fortunately, Johnny had a turn with Wally's listeners.

Lou passed out a pound or two of lira to La Foresta's lonely waiters, and we returned to Rome the way we had come, by the route of the conquerors.

Except for his exorbitant tipping, over which we had no control, Lou was pretty good about sticking to the ground rules regarding money. Until the last day, that is, when Johnny went down to pay for our week at the Cavalieri Hilton and was told that our expenses had been "taken care of."

Had the bill already been paid? "No, not actually." Johnny demanded to see the manager. The manager stood fast. Lou must have distributed thousands around the place! Then The Flanker, who deplores a scene, decided "when in Rome . . . " and worked himself into a rage. "Look," he said, "I am in the television business back home in Chicago [true]. Signor Malnati owns a chain of restaurants in Chicago [true]. His restaurants pay for advertising on my television station [false]. It is illegal and immoral for him to do me favors such as this!"

"I'm sorry, Mr. Morris, but Signor Malnati insists . . . "

"Signor Malnati is dangerous . . . He is doing me harm . . . DON'T YOU KNOW? THIS IS WHAT WATERGATE IS ALL ABOUT!"

That did it. "Watergate" was the magic word. Johnny won the Big Round, and the poor ol' Pizza King had to go home with money in his pocket.

When we arrived at Leonardo da Vinci Airport to catch our plane back to the kids, we discovered that our Jugoslav Airlines flight had not yet left Belgrade. The plane took four hours to fly from Belgrade to Dubrovnik to Rome—and another hour to fly us back to Dubrovnik. Johnny and I talked a good deal about Lou and Jean and hoped that the recent intrusion of cancer into their lives had been forgotten for at least a few moments during the week.

Not long after, in that same building at Leonardo da Vinci Airport where we had sat and waited for our JAL flight, 18 people were killed by indiscriminate machine-gun fire when terrorists hijacked a plane.

It was that kind of year in Europe.

Josip and Dan were waiting for us at the beautiful little terminal in Dubrovnik when we arrived. As we drove home to Cavtat, the two of them related *their* week's adventures. We could tell that Dan and Josip, some 15 years Dan's senior, had developed a new respect and rapport.

There were still patches of snow on the ground. The kids had had a cold week. Tito had instituted a new energy-saving policy. The country was divided into small districts, each with power on for 24 hours, off for 12, in alternating districts. On the off day, we would lose power at 6:00 A.M. and it would be restored by 6:00 P.M. If you wanted to stay up till midnight, you might have just about enough hot water for washing the dishes and for two people to take showers. The Yugoslav stove, built for power-outs, was only half electric; the other two burners would operate on bottled gas. Trouble was, Dan said, Dubrovnik had run out of bottled gas. Early every morning, Dan had lined up with other citizens to fill gas bottles for both the Robic and Morris households. So far, no luck.

Despite the travail, the children had thoroughly enjoyed their week alone in Cavtat. They had taken turns driving into Dubrovnik with Dan to do the marketing. Deb had done the cooking, and both the big kids had helped Tim and Holly with their lessons. The villa, when we arrived, was spotless. I needn't have worried. One of the best things we did during the year was to leave the children to fend for themselves in a foreign land.

On our last day in Cavtat-Dubrovnik we went to Orsan for lunch. We hadn't gone there often because it was an expensive restaurant, but the best on the Adriatic—and we wanted to take the Robics somewhere special. *Orsan* means "boathouse" in Yugoslav and that's what the restaurant is—a 400-year-old boathouse about 12 miles north of Dubrovnik and carved from a stone bluff. Niko Guerovic was the owner of Orsan, and the property had been in his family for generations. We feasted upon raw octopus salad, the meat purchased from fishermen who rowed to Niko's front door daily. There were delectable scampi and greens fresh from Niko's wife's garden. The wine was superb.

We kidded Josip about what a fine capitalist he would make, and he told us how much he loved Yugoslavia and President Josip Broz, whom the world knows as Marshal Tito. We'd seen Tito recently on television. Anwar Sadat of Egypt had been paying court in Belgrade, and the film had shown 84-year-old Tito bounding down the steps of a building, jumping behind the driver's seat of a big black car, and the old man himself driving Premier Sadat off to lunch. Macho Tito. Josip loved that.

Josip also thought we were very wrong to criticize President Nixon over the Watergate scandals. He asked, "Why does he [Nixon] permit this Watergate?" meaning the political and press attacks. In this, Josip typified the naive misunderstanding of the American political system that we found throughout Eastern Europe, and especially in Russia. The rule of law above the rule of man was vague to some, incomprehensible to others.

As much as he deplored his cruelties, Josip thought that Joseph Stalin was, like Tito, a man for his times and would eventually be revered by historians. And as much as he admired the achievements and material success of his Western friends (and he had many good friends on "both sides"), Josip strongly believed that democracy would destroy itself. "There must be a firm hand," he said. "Otherwise each man says 'I want.' And he finds a way to get it."

Josip acknowledged that there was internal trouble in Yugoslavia because of historical differences between various cultural and ethnic groups and the fact that the rich and poor republics had unequal influence in Belgrade. But he disagreed with Western observers who said that the Soviet Union was just waiting for Tito's death to envelop Yugoslavia's riches—and her Adriatic ports. We couldn't help pointing out that although under Tito a life-style such as Josip's was allowed and even encouraged with selected capitalist incentives, under the Soviet political system a mere directive could put an end to this overnight.

Josip replied: "Because of Tito I have this, and Tito can take it away."

The small children were becoming restless. Little Tammy was snuggling up to Tim, whom she adored. They were tossling their blond heads together. Someday, we teased, Tim and Tammy might meet again.

"What if they got married!" Holly said, making her brother blush.

Josip's ordinarily smiling eyes turned murky and serious, gazing at the child he worshipped. "Tamara will speak ten languages. She will see the whole world and will go to a fine university. She will be free. And then," turning to Dan, "I want her to be like your children, like Dan, when she is his age. To know what she wants and to know how to get it."

And like her father? Josip Robic, a man on a tightrope, a living dichotomy . . . a man of Yugoslavia.

"Vee Vant to Sheeing!"

I suppose it was because we'd driven so many dark nights in the Soviet Union that the trip up the Yugoslav coast in the midst of a blackout was more amusing than terrifying. We got a late start out of Cavtat. Our goal was Lav, a suburb of Split where Josip had made us a hotel reservation. One of the most peculiar sights I recall was a filling station with perhaps ten vehicles lined up for fuel, the dimmed headlights causing the shapes of cars and trucks and the movement of people to cast eerie shadows. There were glimpses such as these, then we would plunge again into the darkness.

The Lav Hotel was super, all right. It could have been in Miami Beach. It had all the accoutrements, including a swimming pool, gym, sauna, sailing and beach facilities, even a Las Vegas-style casino. It was the kind of place "you never have to leave." We wondered if many Americans came to this spot on the Adriatic—and never left.

Lav was illuminated—at least for a while. After an expensive but not particularly good meal in the hotel's continental restaurant, the kids went off to their rooms, Johnny hit the casino, and I went to bed with Alexander Solzhenitsyn (I had by now replaced the copy of *The First Circle* that I had tossed out before entering Russia). A half-hour later there was a big "pop," and the lights went out.

Being fairly accustomed to such events by this time, I wasn't particularly alarmed, and indeed, five minutes later the lights were on again. It was a Saturday night, and the hotel was rocking with local people. There seemed to be few tourists; as a matter of fact, most of the hotels along the Adriatic coast were closed for the off-season. I had just gotten to the place in *The First Circle* where Nerzhin finally wins the confidence of Spiridon and the long recounting of the Russian peasant's travail begins, when "pop," another blackout. This time the kids felt their way to my door, and we all sat and talked, wishing Josip would barge in with some candles—and wondering where in the hell The Dad was.

The Dad, it turned out, was in the middle of a streak. Two hours after *I'd* blacked out, I was rudely awakened by a shower all over my body that amounted to 1,150 dinar (about $75). Johnny reported that he'd had to show his passport in order to gamble. The Yugoslavs, he said, were not allowed to lose their money to the State; this was a privilege strictly reserved for tourists. Nevertheless, the casino was crowded with local spectators. During the first blackout, Johnny told me, he'd just sat there mystified, waiting, because a guy doesn't quit when he's a winner. When the lights flashed on, he saw all the players draped over their money, and the croupiers, too, were enveloping the house funds and chips for which they were responsible. The second time the lights went out, Johnny went native and also dove on his money. He'd had to lie there on that blackjack table for ten minutes. There were perhaps 200 people in the room, mostly immobile, suspended. Then—lights on—animation, as if nothing unusual had occurred. I wondered what would have happened had the event taken place at Caesar's Palace in Las Vegas.

It was raining when we arrived at Kranjska Gora in the Julian Alps, in the northwest corner of Yugoslavia. Never mind the rain, we thought; we would catch up on lessons and do our Christmas shopping. The local people assured us that there was nothing to worry about, any moment now the rain would turn to snow. It must; the entire village (about seven hotels, plus numerous privately owned guest houses) was booked for New Year's, Europe's biggest skiing holiday.

We did the Christmas shopping in one hour and spent $50. That was pretty glorious in itself. Then we turned to cards—five-hour gin and casino tournaments. We ate too much. We had our rental skis fitted. We hiked into the muddy hills and cut our own Christmas tree, then spent more hours making paper ornaments.

Each morning at Kranjska Gora the church bells would awaken us at 7 o'clock, and we'd listen: "Drip, drip, drip." After breakfast we would inquire as to the weather report. "Any moment it will snow," the desk clerk would say. We decided that was the only English he knew.

On Christmas Eve the church bells rang almost all night. Mass was crowded—the village's economy was hanging in the balance. The people prayed. Santa Claus came and went. No snow. On Christmas Day we taught the kids to play bridge.

I don't know why we didn't cut out sooner. The truth of it was, we liked Kranjska Gora. Skiers, particularly young people, arrived regularly from all over Western Europe because Yugoslavia was cheap and because, they told us, the skiing at Kranjska Gora was super. When there was snow. The European kids would move in, sit in the rain for a day, and leave. We met one other American, a lady who'd bought Kranjska Gora as part of a one-month package tour. We never could quite follow her logic, but somehow Tito was to blame for the rain. We wanted to believe her, because we knew that at any given moment Tito might change his mind.

After two weeks in Kranjska Gora, I woke up one morning and without stirring lay utterly relaxed, listening to the music of the church bells blend with the falling rain. Suddenly there was an irate shout in my left ear: "What in the hell are we doing here?" I opened one eye as Johnny, who was bolt upright, looked over at me. "Let's get our butts in the Beast and over that pass into Austria. They close the road when the weather gets rough," he said. "And you never know, it could snow any minute."

Our quest for snow took us through several snow-starved Alpine areas, and in each place we would ask of anyone we saw, "Where is snow?" The answer we heard most often was, "The Kitzsteinhorn glacier." There is snow on the Kitzsteinhorn in July; there surely would be snow in January.

And so, on December 31, we arrived in Kaprun, the village that nestles below the glacier. The sign on the front of Kaprun's only ski shop told us in "charming" English that we'd found our kind of resort—unsophisticated, unfashionable.

> We surely have the right skis for you, the bindings will be adjusted perfectly. But remember, whether yur other equipment ist suitable. Do you have ski wax, goggles, head-wear, gloves, warm sockets, pullover, parka, a skibag for little things, spats and more articles of that kind? If you are equipped in that way, skiing will mean joy and recreation. And that is what we wish for each day of your stay in Kaprun.

And that is what we had on each of the 30 days we lived in Kaprun, joy and recreation—and exhaustion and friendship and lots and lots of Weiner schnitzel.

New Year's Eve is not the best time to find a room at a ski resort. But here was where The Flanker truly excelled. Crunching over the beautiful (if only six-inch) snow pack, he went from hotel to *gasthof* to luxury chalet, trying to beg us lodging. We could have slept in the Beast, of course, but temperatures under clear skies were averaging between 10 and 30 degrees; and much as we loved our True Blue home, it was hard to imagine all six of us rising, stashing the cots, breakfasting, putting on six pairs of skis, and still making it to lessons by 9 o'clock every morning.

After two futile hours of pantomime and cajolery, The Flanker stuck in his thumb and pulled out a plum. As we feasted in the Beast on a delicious new Austrian variety of sandwich makings and a sparkling white wine we'd chilled in the snow, Johnny told us that on his first go-around he'd stopped in one hotel, brand-new but not expensive, where the tough Teuton of a proprietor had turned him down cold. However, Herr proprietor had been called to other business, and his apple-cheeked bride and her 15-year-old daughter had engaged Johnny in conversation. Johnny had, he thought, presented our family dilemma with passion, appealing to the ladies' joint maternal instincts. The Flanker decided to return there after lunch; he felt if he could catch the good Frau alone, he could con us a room. He did . . . and he did. Furthermore, we were promised that the minute the holiday crowd left we could have three rooms and breakfast for $5.50 per person.

Our first week in Kaprun, though, the six of us were grateful for one room. It had two beds; one very nice bathroom (and, oh, the ecstasy of a hot tub after those long days of ski lessons); a balcony that wasn't much good except for keeping ice cubes; and a view of the snow-covered Alps and, on that first night of 1974, the fireworks and festivities of the Austrian New Year.

Our month in Kaprun was nothing short of exhilarating. We signed up for lessons at the Franz Prezenger Ski School and would begin on January 2 to fulfill a dream whose realization had been delayed ten years by the risk it implied to a professional football player and four years by the demands of a career in television: *Finally,* we would learn to ski. On New Year's Day we rode the cables to the ski hut below the peak of Kitzsteinhorn. The day was brilliant, and we could see almost to Salzburg, 50 miles away—at least we could see the mountains that sheltered that magic city. Directly below us, expert skiers swung from the glacier's four lifts. Twenty-one days later we would be swinging from those lifts ourselves.

But that was 21 days later. *Four* days later I wrote the following letter to my sister, Donna:

DEAR DON:

I'd better write you today because I don't know if I'll ever be able to write again. Thank God my fingers are functioning—little enough else is. I knew skiing would be cold and I knew it would be tiring— but I didn't know it would be painful. Remember how I've been propagandizing Johnny for years, even during football, trying to get him to ski? Nothing to it, I kept saying. Fun, fun. "Après ski," rah rah.

"Après ski," my fat fanny. "Après ski" I am fit for nothing. Either all my friends who said skiing was sheer delight are liars or these Austrians are running a peculiarly Prussian ski school.

They put Deb and me in the same "adult beginners" class with

Johnny—which I think he thinks is slightly humiliating, being as he's a "great natural athlete" and all that. Tim and Holly are in a class together, and Dan, who had one week of skiing in Colorado last year, joined an intermediate group. We started the day before yesterday with 20 in our class. By yesterday afternoon's session, we were down to 11 and counting.

The first morning, though, before the pain set in, was actually pretty funny. It was like kindergarten. After learning to put on our skis and adjust the bindings, we did sort of a lap. All we had to do was walk, or rather, scoot, around this flat field. Nobody could do it. There was a heavy fog and great gaps kept appearing in our line. Everybody fell several times, some dropped skis, and the instructor kept hopping around rescuing people. Once we lost Johnny altogether. I looked back and he had disappeared in the fog. He sat down in the snow and wouldn't budge. He just couldn't grasp the idea that this sport might not come so easy.

We work—and I mean work—from 9:00 to 12:00 every morning, have an hour and a half for lunch, then go from 1:30 until 4:00 in the afternoon. Our instructor is named Honk-Peter. He's a student in Salzburg and only teaches for the holidays when the crowds are here. It sort of embarrasses me to call him Honk-Peter, so I just call him Peter. I don't know how to spell "Honk" in German but it sounds just like "honk," you know, like a horn. I don't care if I don't call him Honk anyhow, because he calls me Jane.

Peter can ski like hell but he can't catch a ball, which makes Johnny feel kind of good. Our first afternoon—still in kindergarten session—we were on this bunny hill (more like a mouse hill) and next to us there was a real kindergarten class, little tiny kids, not one over five. Naturally these kids were terrific. I think they planted us beside each other on purpose. Anyhow, their teacher, a very cute girl, was having the kids ski down a hill (bigger than ours), and as they approached the bottom she'd throw them a ball. I guess the idea was to make them forget skiing, let that come naturally, while the kids concentrated on the ball. Well, old Honk-Peter, he decided that looked like fun, so he asked to borrow the ball. That's how Johnny found out the teacher couldn't catch. Peter would throw the ball as you were sliding down this truly tiny slope, and when you squeaked to a standstill at the bottom you were supposed to throw it back to him. But Peter kept dropping the ball because, according to Johnny's analysis, he was "trying to catch it like a girl." Johnny would smile this funny little smile when Peter blew the catch. Peter had the last laugh, though; Johnny fell almost every time. It seems that catching a ball is so instinctive for The Flanker that he concentrated too much on the skis.

Johnny and I both had to exchange our rental boots after one day due to blisters, etc. Tim and Holly met us in tears when we gathered for lunch yesterday. They were frozen and exhausted and didn't want to go back for the afternoon session. I knew just how they felt. But we fed them big bowls of steamy spaghetti, and after thawing for an hour they went back. Holly's teacher speaks excellent English, and since Hol is the only English-speaking child in the class, she gets a little extra attention. Holly likes that.

What one should really do, before learning to ski, is to have a lesson on riding ski lifts. They have every kind here, and there isn't one that Debbie doesn't fall off of. Yesterday Deb and Johnny were riding a T-bar together and started fooling around. They were the last pair up the hill, and I, along with the class, was waiting at the top. About 100 yards from the finish, the two of them went ass over tea-kettle, and Honk-Peter made them both sidestep the rest of the way. Held up the class for 15 minutes. Deb was close to collapse.

I'm sorry I can't tell you where to write next. I guess the safest address would be Poste Restante, Athens. I'm sure you remember that Johnny can't decide whether or not he wants to go out to dinner until he gets hungry. I suppose we can hardly expect him to have an opinion on where we should go next. But I think we're going to have a hankering for some warmth and sunshine.

Love to everybody. Missing you . . . missing people, but nothing else. Adore being a bum. Even a ski bum.

Love,
JEANNIE

Honk-Peter was not Honk-Peter after all—nor was he goat-peter, nor saltpeter, two other possibilities that occurred to us—but Hanspeter. Hanspeter was shy, an exception among the Kaprun instructors, who doubled as social directors, arranging parties and get-togethers for their students and other visitors. Whether the motive was to help the village taverns sell booze or to build rapport for their teaching, the effect of all this conviviality was to create an instant, integrated community from an international group of strangers. Over a post-lesson mug of Yeager Tea (a hot and dangerous concoction made of sugar and spice and everything nice, including schnapps and rum), Hanspeter explained that the girls generally called him Hans and the boys called him Peter. He didn't say why. We decided that it would be much less confusing if we all called him Peter.

We shortly discovered that teacher Peter was interested in our fellow student Elke, so interested that he kept our pretty new friend from Frankfurt after school one day for tea and tutoring—and poor Elke ended up with her left leg broken in five places.

Altogether we took two series of lessons, six days each, in Kaprun; and Elke was only one of three of our classmates who broke legs. We visited her several times at the hospital in nearby Zell am See and again five months later, in May, at her home in Germany, where she entertained us royally for two days. Our spring visit caught Elke in the midst of a celebration; she had just had the pins removed from her leg after a third round of orthopedic surgery. Elke tried very hard to talk us into meeting her the following January—to ski again in Kaprun. Nutsy-gutsy girl, that Elke.

At the end of the holiday season, about January 5, Kaprun suddenly emptied. Ski rental and lesson and hotel rates—which had been low to begin with—were cut in half. The teaching staff at Prezenger was reduced from 18 to 5—all men, all veterans.

Our new class was one-third Dutch-speaking, one-third German-speaking, and one-third English-speaking; the English division consisted of two American boys vacationing from a private school near London, Debbie, Holly, me, and poor Johnny, who had fallen short on his qualifying test. The name of our instructor was Helmut. We got that straight right off. Nevertheless, we usually called him "Mr. Greenjeans" since, unlike his blue-uniformed colleagues, he insisted upon wearing kelly-green tights.

Helmut was small and muscular, a 38-year-old-kid, the absolute King of the Social Directors, a leaping, flying, athletic skier. Mornings, as we bent to buckle our skis, he would go around the group, poking butts with his ski pole, shouting, "Hurry, hurry, we want to skiing!" Pronounced "Hoary, hoary, vee vant to sheeing!"

Occasionally, as our class plodded through exercises, Dan and Tim and their advanced group would fly by. While the boys lifted a pole in salute to Helmut (whom they knew well from all the parties), Johnny, standing in line between an uncoordinated kid from Amsterdam and a faded beauty from Bonn, would twist his poles in the snow with impatience. Eventually Helmut suggested that Johnny was ready to advance into the class with his sons, but by that time we were having so much fun with Mr. Greenjeans that The Flanker decided not to leave us.

Looking back on Kaprun, I don't know how we escaped serious injury.

I think it's because Deb's a goof-off rather than a klutz, but she just couldn't handle a ski lift. Not only did she precipitate disaster while sharing chairs or T-bars with others; Debra also managed to cause chaos even when riding alone. She and Johnny pulled the dum-dum trick of our whole skiing experience one day in Kaprun when Holly fell off the bar in front of them. Deb yelled to Holly to stand right in the lift path and they would pick her up! Given the imbalance between Deb's and Johnny's weights to begin with, the unsubstantial configuration of the T-bar, and the short amount of time Holly had to position herself (not to mention six skis, six pointed poles), there were all the ingredients for sure disaster. The three of them ended up in a monstrous heap; fortunately, their ski bindings released, while the bar snapped up to the singing cable. Johnny, with sheer strength, pushed the tangled mass of himself and his two daughters out of the path of the next passenger on the lift—me. I was furious.

Debbie pulled a Mack Sennett trick all by herself a week after we left Kaprun and had stopped to ski for a day in Igls, out of Innsbruck. (Incidentally, Igls was *much* more expensive than Kaprun—busloads of Americans—and *terribly* fashionable.) The snow in Igls was deep, and the run we were using had a straight-up T-bar lift that ran through a narrow cordon of pines. At no place did the lift intersect the ski trail, as many do. In the soft snow, the lift path had become a four-foot-deep rut. And Deb fell off the T-bar. She doesn't know how, but she found herself, face in the snow, sliding headfirst down this ditch as though it were a bobsled run. With her bindings released and skis dragging, she whizzed straight toward the oncoming ski tips of the riders who had been behind her on the lift.

Deb was laughing hysterically, screaming, "I can't stop! Help!" People were bailing off the tow line right and left, like fighter planes peeling out of formation. On either side of the line, the snow was littered with bodies. But Deb was OK. She thought it was funny. This time The Mom, twisted on her own bar, watched from *above* the fiasco. I wasn't laughing.

In retrospect, those incidents look funny—sort of. However, the time we cabled far above Kaprun to tackle the Kitzsteinhorn glacier on our own, the Morrises had a really hairy day. Holly and Dan came close to falling off an icy chair lift when poor Holly's little behind wasn't high enough for the pick-up. With Dan shouting, "Stop the lift!" the chair pushed her off the take-off platform. Johnny practically attacked the lift operator to get him to see that Holly was hanging from the chair, which by then was almost to the first support tower. After a single scream of terror, Hol froze while Dan held her by one arm and she hung on with her other hand, her little skis suspended 25 feet above the snow. Dan yelled that the operator must back the lift *very slowly* since he was being pulled forward by Holly's dangling weight. As they finally touched back down on the platform, Holly was crying and Dan was shaking; but big brother insisted that Holly go with him on the next chair around— and she did. Holly made three runs from the top of the mountain, then went into the restaurant on the high alm and threw up.

My feet were lumps of pain following almost four weeks of changing ill-fitting boots, so I was more than happy to stay in the warm restaurant with Holly. Still, half a carafe of wine in my stomach made my feet feel better, so Deb came in to sit with her little sister, and I tackled the mountain again. I fell down during the first half of the run, which was deep powder, but as The Flanker pointed out, "Mr. Greenjeans would have said, 'Jean, on second part you do wary well.' "

Holly, Deb, and I took the cable car down from the Kitzsteinhorn, while the boys decided to ski the super-expert route to the middle station. The trail snaked below the cable system. For some reason, the trapdoor on the floor of the cable car was open and only barely covered. Just as we spotted the boys a hundred feet below us—specks in the snow—Holly said she was going to vomit again. She was terribly embarrassed, but there was nothing to do but stick her head out the hole in the floor. The boys went sailing by, oblivious to our problem. "Too bad," said Deb. "She missed."

The Prezenger ski school had a tradition—and for all I know it is an Austrian or even a European tradition—but it took me a while to get used to it. All of the class was expected to gather at the bottom of the slope following each lesson, stand together with left skis flat on the snow and the right ones perpendicular, tips in the air, and shout, *"Schi* [meaning "ski," but sounding like "shee"] *Heil! Schi Heil! Schi Heil!"* Then we could limp home.

I made a rather poor entrance into the *Schi Heil* circle on the last day of lessons: I slipped on the final slope, spun like a whirligig, and slapped myself dead across the mouth with a ski pole ... bruised my cheek, knocked out half a front tooth, and came up with a fat lip. The Flanker slapped me on the fanny. "Way to go, kid," he said.

Schi Heil!

Yugoslavia . . . infinite contrasts — old and young,
rich and poor, East and West . . .

our companions
in the market . . .

an entrance to
Dubrovnik's old
city — there is also
a new one.

Tamara Robic. In the closet, she has Levi's and he has
a Hartz 90-Day flea collar.

Holly and her friend never made it at 5:00 a.m.; but any
hour is bargain hour in Dubrovnik's Gruz marketplace.
(Note that The Flanker is about to drop his purse.)

Someday
Timmy and Tammy
may meet again.

Off Dubrovnik—when the signal comes...one more fish for the cat.

Johnny and Lou and Jean Malnati might have noticed the Bernini fountain behind them, had they not been too full of lunch to turn around.

"Joy and recreation" every day of our stay in Kaprun... but you should have seen Deb and Johnny 60 seconds later.

Whadaya know! Everybody's standing up!

Hanspeter was very patient with his star beginner.

We held "school"
in a hundred
different places . . .
here among the
ruins at Navplion.

Dan awaits the Oracle at Delphi.

At so many places
we had the privilege
of being alone . . .

in the stadium
at Olympia . . .

at the Temple
of Zeus . . .

and even in Athens,
below the Acropolis.

Uncle John Jouras shows Johnny his ancestral home, Akhladhókambos.

Mail call in Athens. After six weeks of isolation on Crete, we
sat in Constitution Square all afternoon and read to one another.
Each letter was a gift to be savored. It was like Christmas.

Monoporis Is a Tough Name

You would think Olympia would inspire me to write one or another
of our sports friends, wouldn't you? Not so. Unfortunately, most
athletic programs today have deviated from the original Olympian
purpose. From Olympia I wrote to Lee and Carol Berkson, friends
from Chicago who find their spiritual nourishment in art.

Olympia, Greece
January 29, 1974

DEAR LEE AND CAROL:

*I think of you often and I hope you will forgive me for not writing
more, but in my role as chief correspondent I have had a disappoint-*

129

*ing performance. My diary suffers the most; I can't even correspond
with myself.*

*So we have finally reached Johnny's fatherland, and tomorrow
we will seek out the tiny village near Argos from which his grandfather emigrated in 1903. We know that ten years ago two of his
grandfather's sisters were still living, and Akhladhókambos is a town of
only 1,000 people. A good many must be Monoporises.*

*We had planned to stop for just a few hours here in Olympia and
we are now going into our third day. Such a tiny village with such a
big name! Olympia! The topography reminds me of Sonoma County
in Northern California—the terraced vineyards, wineries, and hills,
mostly rolling but with an occasional crag for character. And then
there are orchards of lemons and oranges (the best we've ever tasted)
and lush vegetation. Although winter, it's acting like early spring
here: The grass is a carpet splashed with wild flowers—the most
beautiful and fragrant a kind of baby iris. There are eucalyptus and
Monterey-type cyprus and huge, towering pine groves.*

*We are the only tourists. We've walked virtually alone through three
museums, and for the very best of afternoons we wandered over the
huge, beautiful, hard-to-grasp site of the earliest Olympiads. Archae-
ologists began the dig in 1831 and they are still at it. We watched
men working on a hillock that could have been leveled in one sweep
by a big machine. But they were taking it down by the teaspoonful.
We had school: Read our Greek history on the floor of Zeus's temple
and, for P.E., ran footraces in the stadium. We had to laugh at the
old Greek guard, whose face was like the stones he watched, when he
indicated to us that the Roman ruins (so recent—100 A.D. or so!)
were not even worth looking at. The Greeks neither put them on maps
nor include them in the mock-ups of Olympia which are on display
in the museums.*

*This is the perfect time to be here, because not only must it be
hot and dry later, but very crowded. There are numerous hotels, but
most are closed now. Our hotel is old, on a hill overlooking ancient
Olympia with modern Olympia behind. We have it to ourselves.
When we asked about a place to eat, we were told there was only one
restaurant with good food open this time of year. We went there last
night. It is run by a family, and the boy, poised and 14, speaks good
English. The rest of the family is friendly and smiling. It was so good*

we returned for lunch today; and again, as last night, we were taken into the kitchen to peek into the pots to see what was available. I couldn't tell you what the Mama did with lamb and spinach and onions, but it was heavenly. We finished eating and were talking to a local merchant at another table when the boy ran across the street to the orchard and brought us an armload of those exquisite oranges. "A present from us," he said. And the man at the next table said, "That is Olympian hospitality." Another guest said that Americans were the best people in the world—next to the Greeks.

After lunch we climbed the sacred hill, Mt. Kronion, which overlooks ancient Olympia and from which you can see the rivers Alpheios and Kladheos come together to form the valley. For a place that must have been visited by thousands, it is utterly unspoiled. It had rained a little in the morning, but the sun was coming out in time to set. Johnny was playing his macho games: "See that pine cone on that big tree? How much will you give me if I can take this pine cone . . ." etc., etc. He never misses if you lay the money. Holly was romping with a dog she has adopted for the duration of our visit. Otherwise, all you could hear were the birds. I've never been to any historical site more evocative. You could almost hear men shouting, chariots squeaking, horses neighing. From 700 B.C.! For almost a thousand years sport reigned in this place.

When you see how art and sport intermingled in the best years of Greek history, you hate to compare it with today. Now we mingle sport with money. You're the expert; in the modern era of art are there paintings or sculptures of any significance capturing the physical beauty of the athlete or the strength and motion of the contest?

Oh, yeah. I forgot LeRoy Neiman.

Within the limits of our intellectual and experiential resources, we are trying to dip the children into both Greek and Roman history. It's amazing how novels have helped. Debbie read Mary Renault, and that has really triggered her interest in Greece. Dan lived with Michelangelo for four days while he consumed the Irving Stone pseudo-biography. Now he keeps harping on Florence. He wants to go to Florence. Now.

If we can ever tear ourselves away—like tomorrow—we'll head for Athens after searching out Johnny's family and then maybe go to Crete. Then back to Italy. We spent two days in Venice on the way here and loved it. It is uplifting (the endless art and riches), intriguing (a city in water), and depressing (because it is clearly disintegrating— almost before your eyes). But we want to go back and spend more time there.

Ciao! (I learned that in Italy. Used to think it was "Chow.")

JEANNIE

Athens, Greece
February 3, 1974

DEAR AUNT SOPHIA:

Johnny always said that he wished his grampa (your dad) hadn't changed the family name from Monoporis to Morris when he emigrated in 1909. He used to tell me "Johnny Monoporis" would be a much better name for a pro football player. He says with a name like that he would have scared more defensive backs. He thinks Monoporis is a tough name.

We've just finished two days in Akhladhókambos, and even if they don't make them so tough around here any more, you can sure see why they grew that way in the days when your folks left for America.

There are no Monoporises left here in Akhladhókambos (which means "place for making good olives," did you know that?). But there are relatives of your mother, Epthemia Jouras. Still, your father's family name lives on because there is a huge and beautiful tract of land overlooking the village called "the Monoporis place."

Akhladhókambos has one school, one store with a cafe in the back, and three churches. It is on the main road from Olympia to Argos, but there are no hotels or other tourist attractions. The first person we met in the village was your cousin, John Jouras! He turned out to be the only one in the village we could find who spoke English. Guess where he learned the language—Chicago!

We spent two days working out a family tree, and Dan is drawing it neatly and will send it along as soon as possible.

On our second day here, John Jouras's wonderful wife, Joanne, prepared a Greek feast for us. And John filled us in on the history both of the family and of the village. Below the village is a broad, fertile plain that rises to mountains on the other side, perhaps three miles away. You can barely see a trail-like road climbing the hill across the way which John said was the route the pillaging Turks used. In the 16th century the Greeks here lived in the valley in a thriving city called Uisiai. Although Greece is too rich in the remains of ancient structures to warrant excavations here, John showed us ruins of the old fortress walls and pointed out the spot in the valley where the city stood. Now there are fields and olive groves, small farm plots tended by the people who, despite the defeat of the Turks in 1821, still cling to the hillside.

When the Turks began to invade, the people left their homes in the valley and built small stone houses in the shelter of the forests that covered the mountain. The forest is gone, but the tiny house of your mother still stands, surrounded by newer homes of stone and stucco.

According to John, five years ago there were 2,500 people in the village. Now there are only a little over a thousand, most of them old. "Where have they gone?" we asked. "To Chicago!" John and Joanne said at the same time. While people of John's generation worked and saved, the kids now, he says, have plenty to eat and think nothing about the future. He employs people on the farm, he says. And if he asks, "Will you be back to work tomorrow?" they say, "Maybe." And maybe they come and maybe they don't. A man and woman can live easily and well on $30 a week in Akhladhókambos.

Those who have left the village to go to America, though, have not forgotten it. About 20 years ago they sent enough money to bring the sweet spring water down into every home and then paid to send electricity to and throughout the village. In 1955 a school and church were built at the bottom side of the village. More recently another Greek-American donated money for a road across the mountain that reaches the homes at the top of the village. We saw only donkeys and horses on the road, though. There are few cars—which is just as well. Gas costs $2.10 a gallon in Greece.

John and Joanne left Chicago a year and a half ago, and although Joanne seems to miss the bustle of the city (and a large part of her family, who live there), John thrives on the life here. "It is where I played as a boy," he says.

As Joanne was preparing our dinner, Timmy, who loves to cook, volunteered to make the spaghetti sauce—for which he has his own Italian recipe. I'm not too sure Joanne liked that but, as she said, "What can I do?" From that time, John began to call Tim "chief," by which I think he meant "chef." There was broiled lamb and home-

made cheese (from sheep's milk) and Greek wine and peas. Also homemade bread and butter. Tim was most anxious about his sauce, as he had to use some makeshift ingredients, but he needn't have been. Just as we all sat down, John said, "Now, we make this good!" and poured all the lamb drippings into the spaghetti sauce. You should have seen the look on Tim's face. But I was proud of him; he didn't say a word. For the rest of my life, the taste of lamb and olive oil will remind me of Greece.

The first Jouras came to the village from "nowhere"—out of the Greek army, after the defeat of the Turks. This man, who was named Antonios, soon became a sort of peace officer for the whole village. At the time there was much chaos and lawlessness, and now that the invader had left, the Greeks were stealing from and injuring one another. So Antonios, who was a big man and carried a weapon, intimidated the bad people and made the village safe for the good ones. Like something out of America's Old West! He even shot a man in the course of fulfilling his destiny.

It was a wonderful thing for all of us to explore the family roots—especially for Johnny.

Love,
JEANNIE

A Town with a Time of Its Own

It was 5 o'clock on a February morning. I stood alone at the rear of the ferryboat as we approached the Cretan port of Iráklion. I could not decide whether to watch the gray clouds float across the moon to the west or to turn toward the blaze of pink and gold that was beginning to paint the east. Which was more beautiful—the cool, austere moon, extra bright in the dawn light, refusing for a moment to give way to its mistress; or the sun, fresh and flamboyant, proclaiming the arrival of a new day?

We spent three days in Iráklion, the home of Nikos Kazantzakis and the Minotaur. Dan and Deb had read Mary Renault's books *The King Must Die* and *The Bull from the Sea*, both dealing with the mythical Theseus and ancient Greek and Minoan legends. After their reading, it was a living adventure for Dan and Deb to trace the labyrinth and explore the Minoan palaces at Knossos near Iráklion. As for me, I had long loved Kazantzakis's work and was curious to find the wellspring of the ardor and anger he expressed as no other. But I must confess that along with historical and literary insights, what we sought in Crete was sunshine.

Because we'd read that the winds of Africa blow warm and dry on Crete's south coast, we headed the Beast across the island. Choosing the seaward route at every turning, we found ourselves late in the day on a mountainous, pitted dirt road that led us to Aghia Galini.

This was to be one of our best homes on the road. A rich mix of humanity living perhaps as simply as one can live in today's world. As you read on, picture Aghia Galini in watercolors, awash with Cretan light, spiced with Cretan fertility . . . a summer place forever.

Galini is a village of perhaps 300 people whose stone and concrete homes climb the rugged mountains covered even in February with green grass, wildflowers, olive groves—and goats. The principal means of transport is by foot and by ass. The braying of donkeys, the bleating of goats, the clucking of chickens, and the murmuring of wind and surf are the sounds of Galini. The people are fishermen and farmers who have come increasingly to depend on the industry we least expected to find thriving in this remote corner of the world—the tourist trade.

As the Beast rolled into the big square that fronts on the sea and is the core of village life, we began to encounter a unique cast of characters that would people our days for the next month—and enrich us for a lifetime. Galini, it seemed, was a poor man's St.-Tropez, a wintering spot for the itinerant youth of Europe. But in all our European experience, we never found a place where the native and transient populations were more thoroughly blended and congenial. Eventually we decided it was because the travelers and their Cretan hosts had two important fundamentals in common: Both were poor, and both equally devoted to getting through life one day at a time, with a minimum amount of effort.

Galini deserves a book of its own, one of those epic novels where fascinating lives are traced for 300 pages, finally to come together for a moment in time that affects each one. The consummate Galini philosophy, a paraphrase of a line from James Michener's *The Drifters,* was scrawled in the john at Zorba's cafe: "Galini is a place where you spend the whole day doing nothing, and at the end of that day, you rest."

You might ask at this point how we could find value in exposing our children to a community of hippies. Well, I'm not exactly sure what kind of a critter a hippie is, but if it means "dirty" or "addicted," it never showed up in Galini while we were there. With few exceptions, our Galini friends, no matter what their national origin, were very similar to us both in background and immediate purpose. We were a bunch of people on extended tours trying to stay warm and keep our budgets from bending out of shape.

I've done a lot of unacknowledged plagiarizing from various family members so far in this tale, but Dan's descriptions and accounts of our 28 days in Galini, set down in a mere ten pages of his diary, are both succinct and evocative. He begins with a paragraph explaining how he was strangely too busy to keep up with his diary, and then he writes:

> I suppose that for me the rest of my life if someone were to mention Aghia Galini, I wouldn't immediately remember the town by the sea, nor will the people I met there come straight to mind. What I will recall is the way we lived in Galini.
>
> Galini, to me, after all, is not a village, but a way of life. Life there is carefree, occupying, interesting, always enjoyable, very active, and never a drag.
>
> During a typical day I will rest leisurely on our balcony, reading or talking to George and Kay, maybe do a crossword puzzle. I will play several games of volleyball in the square. That's sheer fun. I will have a few sometimes philosophical conversations and a few just plain interesting. I will eat good food, which is important because I love to eat. I will enjoy the company of people I like, and try to decide why I don't like the others.

Dan went on to record in his diary a list of Galini's characters—most of whom he liked—which ran almost four pages:

Emanuel the Hustler—Captured us the minute we drove into the square, tried to sell us three rooms in his hotel for 35 dracs each (hot showers extra), dinner at his restaurant, the Pantheon. Never quit trying during whole month.

Humphrey Lascelles—Super surfer, formula 3 driver, Australian who lifeguards in Britain for a living; 28, from Brisbane.

John Burke—Humphrey's traveling companion; utters strange Australian greeting, sounds like "Wall hoy thea" (means "Well, hi there"); loves a good laugh, wipes out innocent Chicagoans at drinking.

Steve—Married Aurora in India; Peace Corps Volunteer there; grew up in New York City; doesn't know what an olive tree is. Hikes a lot. Hiked from India.

Aurora—Small, beautiful; married Steve in India; half Filipino, of broken Harlem family.

George Morel—The mightiest Morel; oldest tourist in town, looks 50 but is 60; gets up early; has (with wife) fourth room of our hotel, the Pallas; is outnumbered in his family by:

Kay Morel—Wife of George; smokes and sleeps late; ought to complain of primitive conditions but doesn't. Very nice.

Sally Morel—First to rescue us from Emanuel and direct us to Pallas; beats octopus; entertains formula 3 drivers; lives with sister in orange VW named Mandy (for mandarin orange, get it?)

Joan Morel—Only 16, good sister and van-mate of above; worries too much about weight; refuses to practice flute or work on studies assigned by high school at home.

Savvas—Greek, from Piraeus; lived in Chicago for ten years; speaks good English; can't decide where to live.

Cathy—Married to Savvas; speaks Greek; dances Greek. Is hung up on Greeks; can't decide where to live.

Dimitri—Son of Cathy and Savvas; five years old; too bright; speaks Greek and English. Can't decide.

Mike McIntire—Operates a Nikon, an orange VW camper (no name), a surfboard—and a pretty wife.

Nancy McIntire—With husband above on one-year honeymoon, gift from folks; beer heiress, always broke, models (looks it); is very frank and loves wine.

Wendy—From London of not-so-great Britain. Bookworm. Weirdest dresser here—goes around in a satin slip.

George—"The Australian," born in Galini. Cooked fish and chips down under before returning with wife and three kids 'cause he says they were called "new Australians," resented, and treated unequal. Knows how to make a hamburger. Runs Ariston, favorite of town's few restaurants.

Bozo—Local boy, a clown who thinks he's going to open a restaurant to compete with Zorba's. Rides a white Kaw [Kawasaki]; has rich American girlfriend.

Jack—Wise guy who likes to team double-decker with Holly for volleyball. Killer when playing alone.

Pat Mancina—Plays "Tarzan" with Dimitri. Hunts leopards; knows North America like a fished-out lake.

Angelo—Italian/Canadian; super-nice; has short temper in volleyball; buys Holly candy bars she doesn't like but pretends to so he keeps buying and she has big problem.

Antonio—Our landlord, also owns tailor shop (patches Levi's for nothing); also runs town bank from tailor shop. Keeps money in cigar box, has never been robbed. Also local folk doctor and druggist. Probably more.

Timothy Desmond O'Keefe—Moldy traveler, on road for 15 years. Drives Land Rover pulling trailer. Organized four vans with him for three-day trek up island to beach at Palaiokhóra. Duffed out when roads got bad. Lousy tour leader.

And on and on Dan goes with dozens more, many of whom I'd already forgotten, but who gave him a glimpse, not only of life in a small town in Crete, but of life around the world. I can't resist adding five more of Dan's characters:

Johnny Morris—Conducts school; plays bridge; should not compete with full-blooded Greeks in drinking *raki* or *ouzo*.

Jeannie Morris—Thinks she is a writer.

Debbie—Tootsie-on-a-diet. As it should be.

Tim—Highly respected Zorba's cashier; plays volleyball with his mouth.

Holly—Town mascot. Prized by Galinites of all races, colors, and creeds. Getting bratty.

Our hotel, the Pallas, was hung over a cliff, with the village crawling down the mountain to our right. Our three rooms were unheated (and toilets unseated). But what do you want for $2 a day? The showers were spigots on the bathroom walls, with ventilation from a hole above. But the kids who lived in the vans in the square envied us: Most of the time our water was warm—and sometimes, if the eight of us living at the Pallas planned it right, at least four could get a hot shower in the same day.

Below our terrace was a donkey trail that led down to a plain a quarter of a mile to our left, where a small river met the sea. Here the villagers had their garden plots, and every morning at sunup a few would ride by. We always knew when an animal was approaching because the donkey of our household, owned by Antonio and his wife, Maria, who lived in the front part of the building, would set up a terrific hee-hawing. The animal lived in the stable directly below our room and would often squeal and kick his stall in the middle of the night. Antonio had the meanest donkey in Galini.

Every day it was a contest between George Morel and me to see who would get up first to put the water on the hot plate for morning instant coffee. George had recently retired and as yet had not been able to break the early habit acquired in a lifetime of hard work. By 8:30 A.M., when the sun was full and warm on our seaside balcony, Johnny would be ready to visit Elias, the baker, as the morning's first load of bread came out of his wood-banked oven. Holly, Deb, Dan, and Tim got up when Johnny returned and the scent of the fragrant loaf wafted through their open windows.

The cliffs around Galini were honeycombed with intact Nazi bunkers and gun emplacements; the village had been a German outpost on the Mediterranean during World War II. Many sons of Galini had been killed for helping the Australian army escape to safety as the Aussies were driven in 1941 from Greece and then from Crete, and there was evidence that the villagers still reserved a strong affection for Australians—and resentment for the Germans. But this latter was carefully hidden because German tourists made up the bulk of Galini's peak season (spring-summer) tourist trade.

Not a week after we arrived, Zorba, the operator of the cafe before which we usually sunned and played bridge, gin, backgammon, soccer, or volleyball, hired Tim as part-time cashier. Tim worked for food and tips (not that Zorba's catered to a tipping crowd). Zorba said he hired Tim because the poor boy was coming in for food so often and also, he told us, "because I liked the way he told me on that first day, 'Keep the change.' " Between volleyball and his job at Zorba's (where, Tim complained, he got off at 10 p.m., "just when the action starts,") and playing backgammon with young people from around the world, Tim was happy and fully occupied in Galini. Holly was, as Dan said, the town mascot. Both kids were conspicuous by their very presence: The Galini school had only first through third grade, and village children their age were forced to live across the island, usually in Khaniá or Iráklion, in order to continue their education.

The town had several daily events that drew both locals and tourists. Elias's first batch of bread always attracted a big crowd. Most of the kids would buy a small, crisp-crusted sesame seed loaf for 8¢. We bought the big loaf for about 22¢. Sometime in the afternoon, from the road at the top of the village, would come the sound of music. A rickety truck with a staticky loudspeaker would snake down to the square where everyone would emerge to buy fresh oranges and lemons, and sometimes tomatoes and cucumbers. The day's most important event, however, was the first one—when the village's only large fishing boat, after filling its nets all night, came in every morning at about 7:30. Most of the village men were just beginning to paint up and launch their boats, which had spent the "winter" months on the square. But the Big Boat operated year round, and the way her heavy engines throbbed you could *feel* her daily arrival; hers was the heartbeat of Galini.

It didn't take Holly long to become well acquainted with the six-man crew of the Big Boat. Every morning a truck would arrive from Iráklion to trade ice for the previous night's catch. After tidying up the boat and themselves, mending nets, and performing whatever chores off-duty fishermen perform, the men would let Holly leap aboard and rig some tackle so that she could fish from the side while they slept below. This was all OK with me until Hol began bringing home an octopus every day. I don't know whether it was the beating ("Nikos told me to throw it 63 times on the square, Mom") or the eating (fried in butter and garlic) that Holly enjoyed more. Either way, I did the cooking.

We did some terribly significant things in Galini—like when

Johnny and Mike McIntire spent two days trying to reconstruct the Monopoly board from memory. They got stuck on the name of one yellow square and claimed they were going mildly mad with frustration. And so on the occasion of Mike's 28th birthday we threw a Greek-style banquet at George's "Restaurant Ariston." Our gift to Mike was a home-baked birthday cake (not an easy thing to achieve in Galini), and, after intensive investigation, we had been able to inscribe upon the cake with grated lemon peel, HAPPY "ATLANTIC AVENUE."

One morning Des O'Keefe said, "Look, you lot [the Australian always referred to the rest of the world as "you lot"], we should get off our duffers and see a bit more of this island, don't you agree?" We agreed, and so five vanloads of us spent several days on a wild, primitive camping safari covering the western part of Crete.

And we had parties, not the least of which was a 12-hour pre-Lenten celebration of the Greek festival of Apocrias. On that day, Dan had his first (to The Mom's knowledge) taste of the grape. ("You can't say no to a native, Mom. All the books say that.") Indeed, the citizens of Galini were dangerously hospitable. Our soon-to-be 17-year-old shot 40 pictures during the festival, logging none. Months later we discovered these to be among his best photographs.

As the Ides of March drew close, and as the suspicion grew that spring was creeping north again, our friends began to depart Aghia Galini. The McIntires had the general goal of surfing in Morocco. George Morel decided to take his women to Turkey where the campgrounds were good, the weather better, the prices cheap, and the women unliberated. Others split for other ports, but many of us agreed to meet again in May for the Monaco Grand Prix. (Only the Morels and the Morrises made it.)

We found throughout Greece that if one chose carefully, one could eat both cheaper and better in restaurants than by cooking. In Galini, we always had our evening meal out ($8 for the six of us, including wine), usually at the Ariston. But on their last night there, George and Kay Morel had promised Emanuel the Hustler that they would honor the Pantheon. Johnny didn't like the Pantheon because he claimed (Emanuel denied it) the cook put retsina (the preservative used commonly in Greek wine) in the food. *I* didn't like the Pantheon because it was full of cats and they had a disconcerting way of jumping on your lap just as your fork got to your mouth.

George Morel was a great favorite among the citizens of Galini. George was very straight, himself, but tolerant of—or at least quiet about—the youthful antics that surrounded him and his family on what was a one-year, and essentially a "hip," tour of Europe. What was captivating about George was his honesty. All that he had—intelligence, humor, prejudice, warmth, stubbornness—was out front. Sometimes way out front.

We'd just finished Emanuel's beef stew, and Cathy had started to plink her guitar and sing in Greek the sad songs of Mikis Theodorakis, when one of two drunk young Germans who had been staring sullenly across the room at our noisy table went over to the jukebox and, reaching behind it, turned up the volume.

Now, if anyone should have objected to Cathy's singing, it should have been Emanuel the Hustler. The songs of Theodorakis were banned in Greece at the time; indeed, cafes in Athens's old Plaka neighborhood had recently been closed and the popular singer Manolis Mitsias arrested by the government of the colonels for featuring just such songs. But Emanuel, like most Greeks, loved Theodorakis—and Athenian authority seemed remote in Galini.

Savvas, Cathy's husband, who was built like a welterweight, moved quietly over to the jukebox and turned the volume down. The German again left his table and turned the rock-and-roll racket back up. The next thing I knew, Johnny had one German pinned from behind and chairs were flying as well as fists. It was an old-fashioned barroom brawl. Nobody was hurt, and the fight was actually pretty funny, climaxed by old George muttering, as he shook a frightened German lad less than half his age and twice his size, "I've waited 25 years to get my hands on one of you bastards." It seemed the Greeks weren't the only ones still smoldering from World War II.

All of this led to an effort at détente, a gala post-party on a terrace above Zorba's overlooking the sea, and by the end of the evening, most of the rancor had melted. Timothy Desmond O'Keefe, who had declared Australia neutral throughout, simply tossed off his last glass of wine, waved, and said, "Good bloody night, you lot!"

The Morels left Galini the following day. As we were about to leave

Galini, Zorba asked us to sign his guest book. But before doing so, I read all that was written in English and lifted one contribution for my diary:

> I left a civilization where the people moved
> faster than a March hare tripping on acid
> running to the carrot store in P.F. Flyers
> and came to Galini,
> a town with a time of its own, standing off Einstein and
> time/space relativity,
> cause we're still in 3-D.
> Aren't we?

Paint "Aghia Galini in watercolors, awash with Cretan light, spiced with Cretan fertility..."

Zorba didn't dress for lunch. He's the one in the white undershirt.

Johnny Morris "should not compete
with full-blooded Greeks in drinking *raki* or *ouzo*."
However, Australians drinking wine are fair game.

Sally Morel, Holly, and
their victim — an octopus.

Holly teaming
double-decker in volleyball
with John Burke.

Kind Kay Morel
with an infant
neighbor.

The Morels and the Morrises at the fanciest
hotel in town, the Pallas.

Holly beating Pat Mancina at checkers. Angelo's up next.

The path led below
the Pallas to the
village fields.
Deb and Holly and
that mean donkey
are returning from
potato planting.

George (without the
mustache) was a
great favorite among
the men of Galini.
Apocrias was
a dangerously
hospitable holiday.

March came, and it was time to launch the boats. Everybody helped.

Fiddling While the Beast Burns

We'd written so many great things to my mother and stepfather, Bottsy and John Hatteberg, about Yugoslavia that they wanted to see it for themselves and would arrive at Dubrovnik's airport at the end of March. So we took the land route north from Athens, crossed the Greek-Yugoslav border, wound through the magnificently-rugged mountains of Montenegro and around a spectacular bay, Boka Kotorska, to the Adriatic coast where, instead of turning north to Dubrovnik, we turned south. Then, whipping a "U" at the unfriendly Albanian border, we headed back up the seacoast, passing through Budva, Sveti Stefan, and Hercegnovi, all super spots. These resort villages were remote, and empty in March. The beaches were lovely.

After picking up Bottsy and John, we went back to the villa in

153

Cavtat, where the eight of us had a warm and quiet week together before my parents split for Greece and we jumped on the ferry to Bari, Italy. Ten days later we joined them again to see Rome together. I don't know when I found time to write the following letter to my sister, but I did. She sent me the evidence.

Sometime in April
in Roma

DEAR DONNA:

This morning I planned to have two hours with nothing to do but write to you, but minutes after Johnny caught a cab to the suburbs to see if Ford of Italy had the parts to repair the Beast, Holly walked in. She's become such a chatterbox I don't even have time to think.

First the good news. Bottsy and John arrived yesterday from Athens in super spirits. They had some rainy days and a dual case of the runnies in Rhodes, but otherwise a fine time in Greece.

After one full day of hunting, Johnny found us cheap rooms near the Spanish Steps. It's one of those vertical pensiones, and the kids are in one room two floors below us. We have a tiny balcony full of potted plants that overlooks the rooftops of Rome and only have to share the bathroom with four other people, so it's pretty neat.

So much for the good news.

On the way home from fetching Bottsy and John at the airport, the Beast finally blew. After all these months of not so much as running out of gas, our Big Blue Baby caught fire in the middle of downtown Rome's Friday rush hour. It was hysterical. I mean, it was a potential tragedy, but funny at the same time. Remember the days back in Palos Verdes when Bottsy used to take us chasing fire engines just for the hell of it? Remember that time when the field near the mayor's house burned and Bottsy was up there fanning the flames 'cause she said there was more than one way to get that creep out of office? Well, it was just like that. Here our transport, our HOME, for godsake, was burning, but at that particular point in time and place and given our general punchiness, the whole scene just made for comical chemistry.

What happened was, we were idling through this terrible traffic, a Blue Tank in a sea of tiny Fiats and Maseratis, and apparently the engine overheated (apparently!). One warning came when the car missed a couple of times, and all of a sudden Johnny was goosing it around this piazza we'd entered and commenting, low, like John Glenn or somebody, "I think we've got a little problem with a wire."

Then Old Mission Control Hatteberg lost his cool, maybe for the first time. "You're goddamn right we have, Johnny," John says. "This vehicle is on fire!" (John always calls the Beast the "vehicle.") Before any of us knew how it happened, we were pulled up to the curb—traffic backing up all around us—and flames and black smoke were shooting out of the grill in front. We were pumping little coffee cupfuls of water out of the sink pump and running around to throw water into the flames—which we later found out was exactly the wrong thing to do.

The fire revealed a flaw in the "vehicle" not heretofore discovered. Most of the engine is under a cowl inside the cab of the van between the two front seats. The cowl is bolted to the floor in four places, and Dan was frantically going through all of his wrenches trying to find the one that would unscrew the bolts. We couldn't get AT the fire! A huge crowd gathered, and Bottsy, able (as she was at the mayor's fire) to stand back and observe the comedy aspects, was laughing one minute and worrying that the car was going to blow up the next. I wanted to crawl back into the car and get a camera, but I figured Johnny would hit me with a wrench if I tried.

The guys stayed pretty cool, under the circumstances. And just about the time they got the cowl off, a little man arrived with a fire extinguisher. His name was Orlando and, unlike his countrymen who were shouting Italian advice, he simply turned on his fire extinguisher and put out the fire. That was 36 hours ago, and Orlando is still with us. He adopted our problems.

Orlando is very short, about 5 feet 2 inches tall, round-faced, and speaks totally fractured English. You will recall that Johnny isn't the world's greatest linguist. He didn't understand that it was English at all that Orlando was speaking. But he did understand—and accept— the fire extinguisher.

So the fire was out. But where were we? Still in the piazza with a smouldering, burned-out engine. I was sure that the Beast was deceased. Orlando, however, seemed to think otherwise. Blinking behind thick glasses, he finally took the unresponding Johnny by the hand (literally!) and led him to a telephone where Orlando called first a tow truck, then Rome's largest Ford dealer.

So here's old Bottsy, who's supposed to be a heart case after having been up since dawn and flying in from Greece, deciding that since the tow truck would take a half hour to get to us, she would have a look around an adjacent art gallery. I know it's screwy, but we were all having a ball. Even The Flanker, especially after he started listening carefully to Orlando.

Time out. Holly has just given me a letter she's written to her friend Ann Mayer, which she wants me to proofread. . . . She's now given me permission to copy it for you:

DEAR ANN,

How are things doing in the good old, GOOD OLD USA? Here is the most exciting thing in the letter. Are you ready? Here it goes. The other day are car started on fire. (actually, are engine) It was from idiling so much. Dumb Roman trafick jams. As you might know, Romans are crazy drivers. Well, now the car is back in a Ford dealer being fixed. But that's say la vee.

Until the Romans are good drivers,

Love,
HOLLY

Have I taken all these pages to say the same thing?

Not only did it turn out that this Ford dealer was a million miles out in suburbia, but it also developed that Orlando was a cabbie. As a matter of fact, as he led Johnny back from the telephone to the car, he was repeating, "You wanta have taxi, Signor?" "Taxi?" asked Johnny, by now discerning Orlando's English. "You know he's been saying that to me ever since he walked up with the fire extinguisher? I thought he was speaking Italian."

Presently the tow truck arrived. It wasn't built for Beasts, we could see that right off. John, anticipating trouble, said he was going with Johnny out to wherever the van was going. Bottsy said it was her first night in Rome and we were having such a good time anyhow, and so why didn't we all go? Orlando said, "You wanta have taxi, Signora?"

By this time it was dark, and for all we knew Orlando had fabricated the Ford dealer, which we determined was about 15 kilometers away; and knowing Italians, we couldn't imagine that the place would still be open. Nevertheless, everybody but Johnny, who rode in the tow truck, piled into Orlando's cab. Twice he had to stop because the Beast slipped the tow hook. All the time Bottsy was saying, "We ought to go ahead, because the place might close and we could keep it open till the truck gets there." Everybody ignored her. Orlando kept yelling out the window at people who tried to horn into the lane between him and the creeping truck. "What is he saying?" Bottsy finally asked. Old travel veteran Tim answered: "Bottsy, for nine months I've been saying, 'What is he saying?' You gotta get used to it."

Then Tim added, "I love what I'm doing and I wouldn't want to be anywhere else in the world at this time; there's just one thing wrong." Having got the attention of us all, Tim paused while we waited breathlessly. "I have to go to the bathroom," he said. Since he was sitting on Bottsy's lap she replied, "I hope you can wait."

After the third stop for them to readjust the Beast on the tow hook, we decided to take Bottsy's advice and forge ahead. Next problem: Orlando got lost. By the time we found the right Ford shop, the taxi and the Beast were pulling up from opposite directions.

It was a huge, spanking modern auto dealership, and absolutely deserted. But Orlando insisted someone was there; he had spoken to them on the phone (but that was two hours earlier). I stayed in the cab while everyone else fanned out to look for a spark of life. Tim was teamed up with Orlando, and together they found a lighted window and an open door. The two of them barged right in on what we learned later was a sales meeting, a roomful of snazzily dressed young men. Orlando started chattering in Italian (John came in right behind and reported all this) while Tim walked directly up to the chairman and asked, "Toilet? Toilet?" with a look of desperation.

Anyhow, the salesmen opened the garage (and the restroom) and let us park the Beast inside and told Johnny to come back Monday— which is today—and that's where he is now. Orlando picked him up *this morning. So far we've invested about $35 in Orlando, but he's worth it.*

. . . . . Dots denote passage of 48 hours, Don.

Just got back from a day at the Sistine Chapel, St. Peter's, the Vatican Museum, lunch near the Fountain of Trevi, then the Forum and the Roman Colosseum. Quote of the day from the old pro Flanker as we entered the world's most famous stadium: "If you've seen one, you've seen 'em all."

The Sistine, St. Peter's, et al, are magnificent. However, there is a point at which I feel somewhat as I do after four days in Las Vegas: glutted, sated, wondering if all those riches are in the right place. Everywhere in Europe you see how great concentrations of wealth— whether the Czars' or the Kings' or the Popes' wealth—have served to underwrite eras of artistic growth and fantastic collections of art. But if you ever felt the paganism of the church, meaning The Church, you'd feel it at the Vatican. It is all magnificent and rightly preserved. But if I remember correctly, Christ didn't even have his heart in carpentry, preferring to improve and uplift the lives of men where they live. And while it's hard to think Jesus would not rejoice in the Pietá, for example, I think if he'd had the whole of St. Peter's Basilica laid on him, it might just have blown his mind.

The Sistine was a marvel, not disappointing, as some had said, except for the loud recorded voice demanding silence (in five languages). The colors of Michelangelo's frescoes do not show up with the brightness you see in photographs, but the total effect is breathtaking.

The local Ford dealers have never seen anything quite like our Ford, but they said they could fix it. The Italians are really screwed up, but they sure know cars. We're hoping they don't get it fixed for two more days as garage space in Rome (if we could find it) is expensive. Our insurance is going to pay for the fire damage. So we figure the Great Rome Fire is actually going to save us a $30 parking fee.

We gave up Orlando as too expensive, but he did give us an education. He says we need him because there is no subway, which is only partly true. Rome has been trying to complete a subway system for umpteen years but, according to Orlando, the diggers keep running into old ruins. "Then from everywhere in the world people come and they go into the ground and they look at the rocks and they say,

'*Ooooooh,*' *and they say,* '*Ah ha!*' *And still in Rome we have no subway.*" *Then he turns around and grins at us and says,* "*But that's OK with Orlando.*"

But there are buses, and we have by now memorized many routes. It only costs us seven and a half cents to go anywhere in Rome on the bus, and we're always running for them. This morning we were tearing for Bus 81 and Johnny got there first but waited till last, and when he jumped on, the door closed and his purse got caught in the folding doors. The whole rear of the bus (all Italians) heard him yell as the doors snapped closed and we took off. Then The Flanker turned to the rear conductor and said very calmly, "*I think my purse is hanging out.*" *Heads swirled, and there he was, up tight against the door with that black vinyl bag you gave us squeezed at the straps and the business part dangling out in the street. Johnny wasn't about to unhand his bag, so the rear conductor yelled something up to the driver in Italian . . . and the whole bus broke out laughing. They stopped the bus and opened the door.*

Well, Don, it's taken me four interrupted days to write this letter. I must say, Rome isn't the most restful place we've visited. But "that's say la vee."

Love,
JEANNIE

John, Bottsy, The Flanker, Jeannie, Dan, Debbie, Tim, Holly.
Togetherness in the Beast.

''If you've seen one, you've seen 'em all . . .''

Pisa makes you punchy.

This is what you call sleeping together.

Yes, we did, we wallowed in Watergate . . . a peculiar nostalgia.

"Intimate dining" is universally prized. We had it every day.

So I've got 'em all out of the Beast. So now what?

Switzerland . . . camping in
exquisite Lauterbrunnen . . .

sometimes it's hard to keep eyes
on the typewriter . . .

in the valley . . .

on the glacier.

West Germany...
Motocross
Saves....

George and Dan
at dawn on
race day...

and the race.

In the midst of modern West Berlin, a stark reminder of World War II.

Motocross Saves

With Bottsy and John along (making eight in the Beast), we continued on our way through Italy to Austria. It was an easy one-day trip from Florence to Innsbruck, and before the sun set we'd found a small *gasthof* with reasonably priced rooms and a menu that made no gastronomical bows to its neighbor to the south. That sounded super to us. We were looking for schnitzels and sauerkraut. Since we had been doing so much sightseeing in Rome, Pisa, and Florence, we had adopted the Italian custom of taking a substantial midday meal in a restaurant. Budget cuisine in Italy is not exactly light and variable. We were pasta'd out by the time we reached Innsbruck.

In any restaurant in Germany or Austria you can always find a big dining table. I don't know what in their culture requires this—

certainly families are smaller than in Italy, where they specialize in tables for two (there's a moral there somewhere)—but whatever the reason, our first morning back in Austria found the eight of us sitting comfortably over coffee with 180 degrees of Alpine scenery stretched below. And "wallowing in Watergate."

We'd been keeping up with the Watergate story, reading every word. We were so far away that it was a kind of running serial for us, a ludicrous tie to home. It was May 13, 1974, and President Nixon had just released those infamous transcripts weighing, according to *Time,* six pounds. It took us three days, mostly reading as we drove; but starting that pristine morning in Innsbruck, we read every ounce of the transcribed tapes out loud. When we finally reached the end, Holly, who had been playing solitaire, drawing, and sometimes complaining about what she called a horrible and dull story, asked, "Mom, what did they write about in newspapers before Watergate?"

I can't remember exactly how many days we spent in the Alps. I do recall that we paid no attention to borders and were at various times in Italy, Austria, Switzerland, Germany, and France. But we were only out of the mountains once, when we delivered Bottsy and John to Munich for their trip back to California. We had near perfect weather for camping. It was a Maytime Alpine wondertour.

The Disney playgrounds of California and Florida must have been in part inspired by the Alps. I'm not talking about Alpine scenery or that papier-mâché mountain in Anaheim named after the Matterhorn; I'm speaking of all those wild Disney rides. It is a wonderful American accomplishment to be able to distill and package thrills so that for the price of a ticket they can be enjoyed in one day. But with due credit to the late, great creator of Mickey Mouse, our visit to the Alps erased all memories of other "worlds" and "lands."

First I've got to tell you that the mountains are not all that's high. It's expensive. The only thing that doesn't cost you is looking, and that's just if you're satisfied to see the Alps from their bottoms. We're "tops" people ourselves. However, we found we could beat the price squeeze by camping and cooking.

In Salzburg we went on the highly touted "Sound of Music" tour, but we didn't find out the hills were really alive until we dove about 1,000 feet *into* one of them. Dressed in floppy white overalls to protect our clothing, we traveled by cable car to the top of the *salz* (salt) mountain. Then, our way lighted only by the lamps carried by two miners who marched before and behind offering humorous (live, unrecorded) dialogue, we returned down the inside of the mountain through almost three miles of narrow, sometimes crystalline, passageways. We made this incredible journey by foot, by ferry over an underground lake, by tram, and, best of all, by means of seven bottom-scorching slides.

From downtown Lucerne, Switzerland, it was a full day's trip, perhaps the ultimate in round trips, to the top of towering Mt. Pilatus. Again, getting there was as much fun as being there. We went by steamer across Lake Lucerne to Alpnachstad to board the "world's steepest railroad" (top gradient, 48 percent), which carried us up 7,000 feet to lunch on a sun-soaked terrace, warm despite the snow-pack it sat on. The trip down—by cable car—involved a virtual dive off the other side of the mountain, with a later switch to smaller cars for a half-hour glide down to Kriens, where it was a 12-minute bus ride back to Lucerne.

It only added to our excitement that the cable-car system quit at one point, leaving us suspended above the wildflowers for an extra half-hour. We spent our time devising miraculous means of escape and figured, all in all, we got double our money's worth in thrills.

Poets have described Lauterbrunnen, so I won't try, except to say that it was an otherworld of beauty, with countless waterfalls leaping over thousand-foot glacier-cut walls to reach streams that crisscrossed the grass-carpeted campground where the Beast and its inhabitants could easily, we thought, have lived happily ever after.

Lauterbrunnen is a popular winter and summer resort, but during those clear, sunny days in May we had little company beyond a few gypsies like ourselves, perhaps a dozen die-hard skiers who were still being airlifted to the high snowfields of the Jungfrau and Eiger glaciers, and the friendly and colorful local farmers with their belled dairy cattle.

By this time we had two orange pup tents, one for the boys and one for the girls, and our camping routine had become instinctive. Going to bed shortly after dark and getting up with the valley still in shadow, the sun touching the sparkling white mountain tops, was my idea of a perfect schedule. We all turned in at the same time, but the kids inevitably slept later, until the sun hit the valley and heated up their little tents and discomfort drove them out. Meanwhile, Johnny and I would have had an hour or two awake, but still in our sleeping bags, sipping coffee, talking, and reading. I loved those mornings.

At this stage of our travels, The Flanker and I would have been content to sit and look, but the kids inspired us to action. Up the valley from the village of Lauterbrunnen and 10,000 feet up again at the top of the Schilthorn sat a revolving restaurant called Piz Gloria. The cable system up is the "biggest of its kind as regards difference in altitude and length" (car capacity a scary 100 persons). Were the kids impressed with the great feat of engineering? Well, not exactly. As we revolved slowly, sipping Cokes in the almost empty restaurant, they relived the hair-raising scenes from the James Bond movie "On Her Majesty's Secret Service" that were filmed on the Schilthorn.

For our part, Johnny and I were watching an old couple who sat a few tables away. They must have been in their 80s; we'd first spotted them supporting one another as they hobbled from one cable car to the next, curiosity and excitement filling their lined faces. We had yet to see this extraordinary pair stop smiling. Just now it looked like she was telling him a joke, and he was cracking up. Beautiful young people are born, they're a dime a dozen; beautiful old people are self-created, and you see one now and then; but a beautiful old couple? Well, you might just have to go to the top of a mountain in Switzerland to find something like that.

During their off-hours in Lauterbrunnen, Dan and Tim haunted the nearby hangar of Air Glaciers helicopter service. So our next excursion was perhaps inevitable.

Climbing mountains is all well and good, but there is a lot to say for darting around them, then zooming toward the edge of a glacier where it looks like a fierce waterfall of ice, and finally (gasp!), with the helicopter changing suddenly from a bullet to a bubble, floating above certain disaster to land absolutely alone at the top of the world. For this experience we couldn't find a superlative (except the price: $100).

Tearing ourselves away from Lauterbrunnen, we stopped in Bern to see the famous performing bears, then went on to Gruyère, still in Switzerland. With automobiles *verboten,* the village was a treat, and a guided tour of the chateau of the counts of Gruyère provided an exciting capsule of feudal history. Down the hill is the famous cheese factory where from 7:00 to 9:30 in the morning we found out how to make cheese with holes in it. It was fascinating and, glory be, it was free!

Dan insisted that we could not leave Switzerland without photographing the Matterhorn, so next we headed for Zermatt. We arrived in Täsch late in the afternoon and took the electric train up to Zermatt (no cars again). Predictions were for bad weather the next day, and we were anxious to have a look at the famous mountain. Hiking through the fashionable village and up into the foothills, we found a grassy knoll and relaxed to watch the sun set on the misty Matterhorn.

The children, of course, were all for sticking around another day and climbing the mountain. It was a grim trick, but as we tore back through the village trying to make the last train down to Täsch, where the Beast was parked, Johnny and I paused to point out Zermatt's equally august mountain climber's cemetery.

Naturally, The Flanker got to the train first and, standing on the step of the end car, cheered us in the stretch. With the settled passengers visibly amused, Dan galloped up carrying Holly on his back. Barely leaping aboard as the train moved out of the mountain station, we once again confirmed our new discovery: In the Alpine world the "way to go" is almost as thrilling as being there.

We went to Cologne, West Germany, for two reasons. First, to keep a date I'd made as a senior in high school 20 years earlier, when I promised my friend Hella Fesefeldt, an American Field Service exchange student, that one day I'd visit her in her own country. Second, we went to Cologne because, according to Dan, Motocross Saves.

Dan's passion for Motocross, dirt-bike racing on a marked course over natural terrain, had begun innocently enough—with a minibike. However, in our family, just buzzing around isn't enough when competition is possible, and by the time we had moved to the farm, Dan had discovered Motocross, a popular sport in Europe but not well known in the States. Non-buffs tend to lump all motorcycles together, usually under the heading "bad." But Motocrossers consider themselves a breed apart; they look down on Hell's Angels and even consider Knievel evil because he tarnishes the pure sport and bad-raps the bike.

Johnny had never been much for sports that didn't require balls. But he made two concessions to Dan's flaming interest in dirt bikes: Dan could use the money he earned as our exclusive photographer on the trip to buy a 250-cc. Honda Elsinore; and while we were in Europe we would find and attend a famous European Motocross Grand Prix. At the moment the problem was to find a Grand Prix. Summer was upon us; our time was running short.

Poor George Morel, making his 99th concession of the year to daughters Sally and Joan, had consented to join in this adventure and promised to meet us at the American Express office in Cologne at high noon on Friday, June 14. We had figured we could make Beuern, the race site, which Dan had pinpointed as being a little east of Cologne, by that evening.

Meanwhile, we planned to keep my date with Hella, now Mrs. Christophe Van Auer. Hella lived with her husband and two sons in the Cologne suburb of Bergisch Gladbach. Somehow we got into a time squeeze, and Dan was called upon to effect the Morel rendezvous alone. How, when we had had six weeks' notice on the Morel meeting, 20 years' notice on the Hella meeting, and one full year in which to fit *both* dates, we could find ourselves in a fix for time, I could never explain.

Although in telling us about it later, Dan indicated no panic, the fact was that he could find no American Express office in Cologne. There was none, so the Morels didn't find it either. Nevertheless, such were their vibes that Sally and Dan met at high noon at Cologne's central post office, even though no real contingency plan had been arranged.

By the time they met, George was fit to be tied. He was a planner and he had planned on an American Express office in Cologne. And too, as much as he loved his women, George, you will remember, was not overfond of the Deutsche and he wanted to get his butt out of Germany. Kay, by this time, was ready to get hers out of Europe.

The Morels, it developed, had been settled for two days in a lovely campground by the Rhine outside Cologne. Just that morning a local clergyman had asked them to move their camp because they'd settled on the spot where he ordinarily set up his platform for Sunday services. Not wishing to defy the Lord's spokesman, the four Morels had spent a couple of hours that morning moving Mandy, the van, and re-staking their two tents. George had been happy to accommodate the good reverend because, according to the information Dan had given them at our last meeting in Nice, the race was somewhere in suburban Cologne and there would be no more moving for at least two days.

Motocross was Dan's thing, and except for our long-anticipated visit with Hella, we had given over the weekend to his leadership. It had not been until we were approaching the outskirts of Cologne the previous evening that Dan, studying one of several maps very carefully, had ventured in a timid voice that the Beuern we were headed for just might be the wrong Beuern. As a matter of fact, the Cologne area town was spelled "Büren." Dan had located a correctly spelled Beuern. It was near Munich, 300 miles away. Poor Dan proceeded into a mild panic. You could see his heart beating in his eyes. He had only one relatively positive clue going for him—a map of German campgrounds. There was a campground about 100 miles east of Cologne that had a postal zone just one digit different from the one to which Dan had sent for German Grand Prix information. There was no Beuern listed in the area; but Dan decided we should head for that spot anyway.

I don't think anything but their sterling character and respect for Dan kept George and Kay Morel from giving our number-one son the dead eye and hightailing it west for Paris, which was where they were actually supposed to be. The Morels had never even heard of Motocross. And George didn't care for motor sports anyhow.

George hadn't forgotten our last encounter, in Monaco—he had gone hundreds of miles out of his way to meet us that time, too. He'd spent $72 to buy four square feet of grass where he had been permitted to put his own campstools in order to see two yards of the road upon which the Monaco Grand Prix was running. Then he and Kay had settled down to hold the grass plots while the rest of us, operating true Flanker style, had spent the morning in a cafe, watching the Beautiful People, and the hour before the race in the pits, rubbing shoulders with the likes of Emerson Fittipaldi and Elizabeth Taylor.

Ten minutes after the gentlemen started their engines, we discovered that all the guards had deserted their posts to watch the race; so we spent the afternoon wandering from one choice viewing spot to another.

Back at our campground in Nice, and still fuming about the $72 rip-off, George had burned the midnight propane writing a letter to Prince Ranier and Princess Grace. George did things like that. He said he'd never set foot in Monaco again, but he thought he could make the hot-shot principality better for the next little guy.

But a month later, in Cologne, George wasn't the only angry American working up to an eruption. It was all Johnny could do to control himself when Dan returned to our campground an hour behind schedule after meeting the Morels. We would be late for a dinner date of 20 years' standing. With his luck running bad, Dan had gotten mixed up in Cologne's commuter railroad system. The worry about missing the Motocross Grand Prix of his life was being replaced by the fear that he was leading a platoon of people he truly loved on a wild goose chase. Still, Dan was determined to strike out for "Hill #6301," the postal zone of the mythical Beuern. Dan said the military designation had appealed to George, located as our objective was in the heart of Deutschland.

We left Dan sitting on a log outside our campground waiting for the Morels, who had gone back to strike their encampment by the river for the second time that day. They would pick up Dan at 5:00 P.M., head for the agreed-upon campground, then call us at Hella's at 7:30, at which time we would take our leave to join them. It was at Hella's, while examining a detailed German atlas, that we discovered that, with a couple of minor differences in spelling, there were 13 Beuerns in Germany.

Dan called at 7:30 and said he and the Morels couldn't find even one of them. "Find it, damn it, and call back by nine fifteen," Johnny instructed through clenched teeth. "We've been here since four o'clock and we can't impose any longer." "Yessir," said Dan.

At 10:00 P.M. the phone rang again. Johnny answered it. He listened stonily while Dan told him he and George had found the campground in the right postal zone. But there was no Beuern, nobody had heard of a Motocross event, and it was raining. The road we would have to take to find them wound through hilly farmland. I heard The Flanker ask one question. How long would we need to drive to get there? Danny said, "Four hours," and hung up before Johnny could scream.

By this time the wonderful Van Auers were nodding. Holly was about to collapse, and Tim was a solid fidget, thinking about nothing except getting to the race—actually seeing Belgium's Roger de Coster, hearing the scream of America's Brad Lackey's two-stroke Husqvarna, grinding Germany's Adolf Weil's dust between his teeth. Like a fanatic convert, Tim had adopted and expanded on Danny's passion for Motocross.

Worrying about poor George and Kay, who we thought by this time must be consumed with fury, we pressed on. I had about decided that Motocross was a fatal disease, and not only was Dan expiring from it, he was taking the rest of us with him. At 1:00 A.M. we pulled into a parking lot and rigged the Beast for a brief sleep. We didn't know it then, but we were still three hours short of our destination.

At 11 o'clock the next morning, we stopped at a gas station which just *had* to be near "Hill #6301." And there, taped to the window, was a poster. It said, "Motocross Grand Prix—Beuern," and then the magic words, "Bei Giessen." By Giessen! Giessen was on the map! The station attendant gave us the poster.

At noon we found a muddy campground and searched for the Morels' orange van. It wasn't there. Then we spotted George. He was standing in the mud beside the tent which was usually attached to Mandy, holding a steaming mug of coffee. He waved. Then Kay emerged. She just barely managed a smile.

We gathered George and Kay into our van and poured wine and apologies. Dan, Joan, and Sally had driven Mandy into the nearest village to buy groceries and inquire as to the whereabouts of the Great Event (for which the practice laps were to start within hours).

I'm not sure Kay was overjoyed when she saw the huge poster we had hung in the back of the Beast for dramatic impact, but Danny's reaction was perfectly clear. He told us later he had been scared spitless to face Johnny's anger and all of our disappointment. Indeed, when he stuck his head in the van, his arms loaded with fragrant fresh bread, he looked at each of our faces before his eyes riveted on the poster and those international words, "Grand Prix." "You found it. YOU FOUND IT!" There was a little sob in his laugh.

Good old organized George Morel, knowing he was in the right postal zone, had again set up camp. But Giessen was still 30 miles away, besides which the campground's johns were holes in the ground and it was beginning to rain again. Nobody was anxious to stay, so George decided to strike camp again. The ten of us crowded into the Beast for lunch. The wine was good, and Kay began to smile.

As we got "bei Giessen," we began to ask the question, "Moto-cross?" And so, guided by smiles and pointing fingers, we homed in. We never did see a sign that said "Beuern," but we were beginning to see a lot of traffic and many, many motorcycles. Finally, we entered a tiny village and slowed up in front of a young boy who was vigorously sweeping the sidewalk in front of his home. We didn't have to stop. "Motocross!" he yelled, and pointed his broom to where a dirt road disappeared over a grassy hill.

The Beast led as we crested the hill and saw the flags of a dozen countries, the swarming crowds, the dust—and heard the unmistakable whine of the dirt bikes' two-stroke engines. In Monaco the engines had roared. In Beuern the engines screamed. In Monaco the super-rich had lined the balconies and grandstands while others, like George, had paid a heavy price for a mere glimpse. At Beuern the poor and passionate were gathered. Whatever you do at a Motocross race, as the faithful say, "you do it in the dirt." There is something especially clean about that.

The sun was now shining, and a slight breeze carried the dust through the flags. As we approached a railroad-type gate, Johnny saluted to the officials, who waved and raised the bar. We slid through and drove up the hill toward the judges' tower that dominated the center of activity. Behind us we saw the gate fall in front of Mandy. With George's luck, we found out later, the German guard had even said, "Halt." Deciding to worry about George later, Johnny kept the Beast moving past the grandstand and up to another gate. A group of girls was standing nearby, and Johnny signaled them to raise this barrier. They did. We rolled on past the pits, into the camping area—and right up to the track, which streamed in and around a beautiful grassy hill studded with oak trees. Tim was ecstatic. "Dan!" he cried, "THERE'S DE COSTER!" Roger De Coster was

Tim's version of Johnny Bench and Joe Namath rolled into one—a superstar.

But Dan had something else on his mind. The minute he knew we were "in," he leaped out of the car and went back to help George. It was a full kilometer's run down the hill.

George had no problem, really. By paying 32 marks for four tickets (for the two-day event), he got through the gate. An hour later, Johnny had conned two press passes and conducted George and Mandy out of the public parking lot and up to our exquisite site on the grass beside the track. Two days later, George was still asking Johnny how he "does it." Johnny didn't have an answer, but I do: The Flanker has all the moves.

We were all scroungy from a night on the road. We'd planned to "hotel it" in Beuern, but we weren't even sure there was a Beuern, much less a hotel, nearby. I had to hand it to Kay. She actually spearheaded the move not to leave the track. So we circled the wagons, pitched the tents, quickly inventoried and pooled our groceries, and settled in for the weekend. Dan began a studious effort to educate his covey of skeptics in the art and sport of Motocross. In honor of meeting the Morels again, we had invested in a bottle of vodka. In honor of seeing us again, the Morels had bought a bottle of vodka. We had an honor-or-able cocktail hour and banqueted on charcoal-broiled sausage, heaps of rice, fresh fruit, and bread and wine. We had thought we wouldn't have enough food for all of us for the weekend, but it was the loaves and fishes all over again.

Only once before in Europe had we found a campground where open fires were allowed. This, of course, was not a campground at all, but a race site picked out of the farmland and chosen, it seemed, for its extraordinary peace and beauty. It was sunset as the noisy practice wound down, the spectators left, and the pit racers turned their attention to the abundant good German beer. Fires sprang up among the vans and tents that were scattered over a ten-acre area near the track. After dinner, people began to gravitate to these fires, which were fed by large stacks of wood that had seemed to materialize from nowhere. The stars were close enough to touch. There was no electric light anywhere. The scene resembled nothing so much as an ancient military encampment.

We saw more Americans in Beuern than we had seen anywhere

else, each and every one of them a GI or "dependent." We joined the fire nearest us, where a group of about 30 people, half of them Americans and half Germans, laughed and sang. The catalyst was a German boy named Karl, long-haired, lanky, and a natural comedian who entertained in both German and broken English. He made us tell our names and where we were from and wangled a laugh with each response. Occasionally I would notice Dan making a survey, just to be sure we were all having enough fun.

Tim and Holly retired to their pup tents first, then George and Kay; finally Johnny and I walked the 20 paces over to the Beast. We washed as well as we could and zipped our bags together and relaxed, breathing the fresh June air tinged with campfire smoke. Next door Karl was leading the group in a garbled version of "Dixie." We didn't mind the noise. In fact we found it convenient.

Dan was sustained throughout the weekend on pure excitement. He ate little and slept less. On the Big Day, I awoke at dawn and pulled back the curtain. Beer cans were neatly stacked by still smouldering fires. I saw two people: George, puttering beside Mandy, trying to quietly stir up some coffee without awakening Kay; and Dan, far away where the track turned into the trees, walking alone, kicking the dirt, then looking toward the east, where an orange sun was telegraphing its eminent arising. Race day was going to be perfect.

Dan convinced me. Motocross is a fine, exciting sport. A Grand Prix consists of two "motos," each 40 minutes plus two laps. Every track is different in its demands, and each foot of dirt presents a new challenge to the rider. The terrain dictates "jumps" (a mound followed by a ditch), "whoopdies" (wild little bumps), "berms" (soft ridges of earth on turns which the rider must take in a position almost horizontal to the ground), and of course hills and hairpin curves. Many riders don't even finish the race. Spills are violent and dramatic, but fortunately not nearly as dangerous as they look. The bike has a tendency to go one way while the rider goes another. Most landings are soft.

Although one of the best views of the race was from the tables and chairs we set up at the back of the Beast, we still clambered the mile or so to see every test of skill the track presented. One of us always remained at the van to keep a tally sheet of current standings. We switched the press passes around to give everybody a shot at either a start or finish from the tower. When Kay was questioned about her credentials by the guard at the entrance, she told him angrily and with great authority that she was a sportswriter for the *Chicago Tribune*. The doorkeeper stepped aside with a bow of respect. Kay had joined The Flanker's club.

Riders receive points for every finish up to tenth place in both motos. The points are lumped together, and an overall winner is declared. The Beuern winner was Adolf Weil of West Germany, so the natives were happy. So were we. Happy and hungry and dirty, our hair gray with dust, we formed up Mandy and the Beast and moved out to find a town that was on the map—a town with a hotel and a restaurant.

It was months later when Gary Pearson and Steve Madsen, two of Dan's closest friends and fellow Motocrossers, showed me the letter Dan had written shortly after our wild weekend in the heart of Germany. This is how Dan's letter ended:

For me, the greatest thing about the weekend was not the fun we had or the excitement of the races. It was the knowledge that everyone else had a good time. My mom, dad, Deb, Tim, and Holly, Sally, Joan, George, and Kay all thought that Motocross was one of the most exciting sports they had ever seen. A couple of days before, when I was leading everyone around central Germany for a race that wasn't known or cared about, I thought, "This is really going to be a bummer." They were going to hate the whole thing. But they didn't. You know what happened? Very simple. Motocross Saved.

In a most unpromising little village we ran across a brand-new, totally sterile, modern motel. Normally such a sight wouldn't turn any of us on; but when you're dirt from teeth to toenails, sterile is beautiful. With the Beast leading, we pulled up in front.

"What do you think it'll cost?" George yelled across as he pulled the orange van abreast.

"Let's find out," Johnny answered and quickly mopped the most conspicuous dirt from his face and hands with a wet towel, whispering at the same time to us, "I don't care; I'll pay it."

Then Johnny and George each grabbed Holly by a hand and disappeared into the building.

Holly and her companions were gone for a half-hour, while the rest of us sat and starved. Johnny said later that he'd had a double problem, the first being that the owner-manager-chef was "hard-nosed," not the kind of German George was likely to cleave to (or even tolerate). The second was that Johnny was determined not to move on and so, in order to persuade George, engaged in a persistent bargaining session.

They started with two rooms (the kids would stay in the vans) for 48 marks ($20) each. The bottom line was three rooms, two for 38 marks apiece and *"ein mit kinder"* (pointing to Holly) for 35. Johnny also promised the proprietor we would buy dinner in the motel dining room. When Holly, Johnny, and George came out to consult the rest of us, we voted aye before they got a word out. Holly and Tim would sleep inside; Dan and Deb, Sally and Joan would sleep in the vans. All ten of us were literally itching to have showers—and quick.

The motel had what a real estate agent might term a miserable traffic pattern (for our purposes). Theoretically we had access to two showers on the second floor. But the motel's only door swung directly into the front desk, guarded constantly by the dour proprietor, and the route to our rooms above lay directly through the rather nice dining room, which was beginning to fill with well-dressed Germans. Pooling our rapier brains, we devised a plan whereby all ten of us would sit down to dinner and order drinks; then those who'd be staying in the vans would wander, two by two, upstairs to de-dust themselves. The timing was perfect, but we knew the proprietor was on to our scheme when, now as maitre d', he came to take our dinner orders, then turned a stern and deliberate gaze on the damp, lanky locks of all of the teenagers. Naturally, everybody had had to wash their hair.

The food and wine were excellent, and the total price for a three-course meal for ten was just $40, and that included two liters of excellent wine. So, brimming with new-found spirit, George dragged Johnny to the kitchen to shower compliments on the chef who, whipping off his apron in a Clark Kent switch to his proprietor role, lowered our room rents to "35 marks, same as for *kinder,*" in an apparent gesture of international good will.

With the sudden melting of the Teuton, George decided to tell one of his favorite Hitler jokes. Those of us remaining at the table, of course, knew nothing of what was going on, but we could hear the kitchen noises punctuated by loud Heil Hitlers. Kay looked across to me and in her calmest, most ladylike voice said, "You know, Jeannie, I do believe that's George." It was—and Johnny said later that he had been a little leery of George's approach to détente. We had learned that jokes are poorly understood in a second language, and English for our host was a very sketchy second language indeed. He'd learned it in an American prisoner-of-war camp.

But the German had the last word. When *his* turn came, he told Johnny and George that in his opinion not a hundred years would pass before Adolf Hitler became the greatest of German heroes, "like Napoleon in France and Mussolini is becoming in Italy." That's what Josip had said about Stalin. It was probably true.

The next morning, the orange Mandy and the Blue Beast split for the last time at a branch in the road. The Morels headed west to the familiar delights of Paris. The Morrises headed east to the fascination of Berlin. "Why would you want to go *there?*" was George Morel's final and altogether appropriate question.

An American sergeant at the Allied checkpoint near Helmstedt, where we crossed into East Germany on the Berlin autobahn, had the same question. "Don't know what you want to go to Berlin for, but since you do . . . " and he reeled off a list of limitations and warnings so automatically that I expected him to end with, "This is a recording." Having done his duty, the GI, who evidently hadn't had much traffic to deal with that day, added some advice of his own. "Listen," he said, "they hate Americans in there. And Berlin is nothin'. There's nothin' to see or do." Then he warned us not to buy the East Germans' "lousy gas" because "it'll ruin your car." He said that a few meters up the road we would meet the East German guards, and "they'll really stick it to you, six marks for the car and six for each person." He warned us that although the East German mark was only worth half as much as the West German mark, the "Reds will only change it even up."

George Morel might have had some satisfaction knowing that there were moments when we, too, wondered why we were venturing across the most fortified and fearsome-looking frontier we had yet seen in order to visit—no, not to visit—to *experience* Berlin.

It turned out that the good sergeant was participating in another case of big-power overkill—or perhaps East Germany was like Russia and tourist control varied remarkably with the whims of the State—for, untrue to his warning, the crossing was mild enough. A female soldier laughingly asked us in pantomime (submachine gun-style) if we had any guns, while another courteous guard processed our passports. It was the busiest border we had crossed, being one of the three ground umbilicals feeding Berlin from the West.

It looked like someone was expecting even more traffic. We could see that a brand-new steel-and-concrete border station was being built, perhaps ten lanes across with innumerable toll gate-like openings, palpable reaffirmation of the German schism. Winding into the woods and farmlands on either side of the highway went the vicious line of floodlit fence with its mined sand—a no-man's-land. Somewhere, resting quietly, we supposed, would be the dogs. The East-West German border, dividing brothers of the Fatherland, is the longest fortified border in the world. We could hardly believe that another frontier could look more formidable—until we saw this border's infamous cousin, the Berlin Wall.

Berlin wasn't that much fun for us, but it was important to go there. We talk about it now in confused flashes. Unlike other European cities, West Berlin leaves a vague visual image; it looks too much like an American city—a new American city. Because of this, one relic left to remind us of World War II, the blackened tower of the Kaiser Wilhelm Memorial Church, stands in stark relief. As for the rest, well, we remember the blocks of sex flicks and porno shops, somehow presented more obscenely than in Paris or Amsterdam. And Johnny, especially, has not forgotten hoofing it two miles with a huge bag of laundry, because not *everything* is as convenient as in the United States.

We loved attending a World Cup soccer game (*fussball* in German) in Berlin stadium, even in the rain, but couldn't help thinking about what it must have been like in 1936 when Jesse Owens won four Olympic gold medals on the field stretched below us, while above Der Fuhrer must have seethed in anger before finally striding out.

After the game we fled for the nearest bus to escape the rain. We didn't know where it was headed, but figured we couldn't get too lost in Berlin since there's a wall around it.

We wandered into a restaurant on Kantstrasse, a place that reminded us of an American family restaurant. But as we finished our early meal, we watched the lonely, not-quite-young set of Berlin wander in to sit individually at separate tables to order a single bottle of wine and survey alternately a third-rate combo and the other solitary yearners.

As Johnny and the kids and I got up, we passed a blond in feathers, sitting alone, an apparition from "The Blue Angel." Tim put his arm around me, as he often does, because he is very affectionate and because he long ago adopted all the social conventions associated with masculinity. The disarranged blond looked at Tim and then at me—and I could see that she hated us.

None of us, of course, will ever forget the Wall or crossing it for a brief and somewhat boring tour of East Berlin. We could barely pry the children loose from the museum at Checkpoint Charlie, so devastating was the impact of the history of Berlin divided.

But if you really want to get the feel of Berlin, try weekending with the Berliners.

There were few foreign visitors in our campground. Almost every tiny *campingplatz* was the weekend or summer home of a Berliner. There are three or four of these campgrounds in the parks on the city's edge and they are jammed with Berliners searching vainly for the countryside. The Germans are a clean people, and a strenuous attempt is made to keep up the facilities, but the summertime population overwhelms by its sheer numbers. Along with the Wall, the sweating and crowded perimeter brought home to us what the reality of living in West Berlin must be.

We were all surprised at our relief on recrossing the border into West Germany. We didn't know whether the tension we'd felt was ours or theirs, but we knew it was real. During our three days in Berlin we found out what John Kennedy meant when he challenged the naiveté of the West by saying: "Let them come to Berlin."

A week later we were in Amsterdam and its immediate environs, which is to say, the Netherlands. Amsterdam is a good city for children; indeed, the average age of Amsterdam's thousands of tourists looks to be about 19. For two or three days we camped in all the places you're supposed to see in Holland, sampled the cheese, gazed at the tile and porcelain; Tim even stuck his thumb in the great straw-covered dike that holds back the Zuider Zee near Edam.

Tiny Holland taught us a lesson in land use. Whatever was not a tilled field was a blossoming park, whatever was not a park was a vegetable patch, whatever was not a patch was a pasture. Whatever was none of the above was under water—and usually in the process of being reclaimed. It seemed to us that if Americans ever committed themselves to use land in this way we could free great stores of food for the hungry world—as well as knock our own prices down.

We were about 48 hours from departure for the U.S.A. when we stumbled on a McDonald's hamburger shop in downtown Amsterdam. Tim's eyes grew to saucers. "Oh," he moaned like a sea captain contemplating shore leave, "it's been so long!" But then Tim did a strange thing. He refused to eat. While the rest of us munched hamburgers and french fries, Tim just sat there, looking upset but breathing deeply, seeming to savor that special McDonald's aroma.

It wasn't until several weeks later, as the six of us spoke about our travels to a Chicago women's group, that Tim finally explained what happened to his appetite in Amsterdam. In answer to the question, "What did you find most troublesome on your trip?" Tim spoke up without hesitation. "The food," he said. "Hardly any place has hamburgers."

Deb wasn't going to let that get by. "Then, why, Tim, if you were so starving, didn't you eat the hamburgers in Amsterdam?" she asked incredulously. Holly was sitting on the panel between me and Tim, not digging this sort of exhibitionism; she had so far refused to talk, but I heard her whisper to her brother, "Hey, Tim, you can say you don't remember, you can say you don't recall." (So! She *had* been paying attention to Watergate.)

Tim ignored Holly, and with the air of a man who was ready to get something off his chest, took the microphone and patiently explained to Debbie and the audience that he had been "keeping a swear." Tim revealed that in Europe he had developed a troublesome habit of vowing, or "swearing," things privately, and that some of his "swears" were "really hard to keep." For example, he had said to himself, "Even if we *do* find a McDonald's, I swear I will not eat a hamburger until I can eat an American hamburger." Tim had told his grandmother, Bottsy, about this secret swear and invited her to be the one to take him to McDonald's for his first hamburger when he returned to the United States.

"Well, then," Tim went on to the women, most of whom had little boys of their own and were trying very hard to accept his tale in the serious vein it was offered, he was "amazed to discover" upon his return home that his grandmother seemed to have forgotten all about the swear. "She didn't even invite me to McDonald's . . . so finally *I* had to mention it. We went and I sat there in front of her and ate my hamburger, my *first* hamburger! She didn't think it was special at all."

Tim paused, and the audience gave up stifling itself to burst into laughter. Undaunted and still dead serious, Tim turned to his sister. "Deb," he said, "I guess it was a big mistake. I should have had a hamburger in Amsterdam."

Our last night in the Beast was not unlike our first; only this time it was Dutch mosquitos instead of Irish fleas.

It was raining, but as much for nostalgia as for convenience we decided not to pitch the tents; we'd sleep six in the Beast as a sort of farewell gesture. The next day we'd be delivering our True Blue Beast to the freighter that would carry it to the States. (We'd be flying back a few days later.) Except for occasional bathroom runs, we played our usual game of "bumper people," running into each other for the four hours it took Debbie and me to prepare and serve our last supper in the van. I made a meat loaf for Tim and hot stuffed peppers for the rest of us. Deb baked a cake, and we broiled tomatoes with cheese. We had a salad with crisp greens and hot, fresh bread and chilled wine. It was a good evening.

The girls were tackling the dishes as I grabbed my towel and soap to leave for the shower room. "Shut the door," Johnny yelled before I opened it. Damn those mosquitos.

There was no one else in the squat, scrubbed, gray concrete building as I stepped into the single shower stall. One of the five languages printed on the sign by the shower was English, and it told me that for a half-guilder I could have 12 minutes of hot water. That was more generous than most. I began to think of all the places I'd bathed during the past year and how I'd been surprised to learn I was always warm after a quick, cold shower and a hard toweling. But this was nice.

The rain was still falling. On one side the shower wall was only a little taller than I, and at the top where it opened to the outside a pink flowering tree thrust a small branch into the warmth. Occasionally a raindrop mixed in with my shower as the breeze stirred the fragrant foliage above my head. Twelve minutes of hot water. That, my friends, is luxury.

Ever Onward!

This tale has had no idle purpose. I'm happy if you have been entertained, but I had a little more in mind than that. I have become a proselytizer, an evangelist, an advocate. I want you to do what we did.

No. It is not impossible. Chances are that if you are the kind of person who has bought this book and read as far as this page, you are in a position to follow in our footsteps, not to mention making a few tracks of your own.

Yes, we spent $30,000; I think it's important to be honest about that—and that's a *lot* of money. But we didn't need to spend that much. Our friends the Morels got by on half that figure, and many people we met on the road lived on even less. I defy anyone to dispute our conclusion that the less money you spend in a foreign country, the more you learn. Money allows you to eat with the tourists rather than the natives, to hire a guide instead of exploring your own routes and interests. Money has a tendency to protect you from the facts of life. It turns the traveler into a spectator when the most lasting values are to be found as a participant.

Take our experience in England, for example. It was our first stop in Europe; we hadn't our bearings yet, so relative to our budget, we spent a small fortune, stayed in stuffy hotels and, in a sense, bypassed the British altogether.

Our year in Europe—August 1973 to June 1974—overlapped Henry Kissinger's "Year of Europe." Remember that? The Europeans were convinced Henry had forgotten. There were major tides swirling through the world at that time: East-West détente, Watergate, the Yom Kippur War, Arab oil embargoes, energy crises, rampant inflation. Almost every Western-block country we visited had a dramatic government emergency or change of administration. By contrast, the Eastern European countries, including and especially the Soviet Union, were frighteningly stable. The ripples from these tides affected us as they did everyone else, but not as severely as you might expect.

So-called crises always decrease tourism. Americans read that the Irish Republican Army is letter-bombing London or that students are rioting in Athens and decide Europe is dangerous. Believe me, Europeans think Chicago is the most dangerous city in the world. They know the street crime figures; they remember everything from the St. Valentine's Day Massacre to the 1968 Democratic National Convention. As a matter of fact, Chicago *is* more dangerous than any city we visited in Europe.

My point is this: Headlines are not representative of ordinary people anywhere. One can get along; and in some respects, times of crisis are times *to go*, not times *not to go* to other lands, especially if you follow the grass-roots route. Difficulties bring people together at fundamental levels. Dialogue increases. As visitors we bought bread from our hosts, broke bread with our hosts, and together, complained about the price of bread.

And another thing. Only once, during a short-lived, Viet Nam-inspired incident in Galini, did we encounter anything that could be described as prejudice against Americans. Throughout our entire month in France, where we'd been warned a frost would surely set in, where we spoke barely a word of their language, we never met a nasty Frenchman. I would like to think the friendliness we enjoyed everywhere was for Americans, but I suspect it was for people, just for people.

We didn't take this trip just for the children. Johnny and I and the kids, especially Tim and Holly, will probably forget a good percentage of what we learned. But what a store of feelings, impressions, and visions our children have upon which to build not only knowledge but understanding of the small world they must cope with in their lifetimes. At the very least, by traveling across the North Atlantic they learned how far is far; in Olympia, Greece, they felt how old is old; in the Soviet Union they discovered how free is free.

Living as we did was very occupying, but it was not distracting. There was time to turn inward—into ourselves, into each other, and, not the least, into books. It was so good for all of us to read and to talk about our reading. The Flanker didn't even seem to miss the sports page.

I don't mean to sermonize, but, as Mr. Greenjeans used to say up on the slopes at Kaprun, "I'll tell you once more time": You *can* escape, and escape is healthy. A whole range of problems, both personal and practical, dissolves when you turn your back on the pressures of ordinary life. The idea is to keep moving; that way the dust and clutter of modern civilization have no time to settle on you. Your major concerns become those of your ancestors: to find food and warmth and to share with your loved ones. You return refreshed, knowing your roots are still there—because you reached them.

Now I must admit that in addition to convincing you to consider the Morris formula for temporary escape and permanent enrichment, I had a second purpose in writing this book. You see, I'm getting paid for it. And I have this great idea that I think I've just about got my gang talked into. With my first check we're going to start a bank account and call it "The Freedom Fund."